KU-666-335

LIVERPOOL

PACKED WITH INFORMATION ON THE REDS

FACTFILE
LIVERPOOL

This edition published and distributed by Parragon, 1998

Parragon
Unit 13-17 Avonbridge Trading Estate
Atlantic Road
Avonmouth
Bristol BS11 9QD

Produced by Magpie Books,
an imprint of Robinson Publishing Ltd, London

© Parragon 1998

All rights reserved. This book is sold subject to the
condition that it shall not, by way of trade or otherwise, be
lent, resold, hired out or otherwise circulated in any form of
binding or cover other than that in which it is published and
without a similar condition including this condition being
imposed on the subsequent purchaser.

ISBN 0 75252 551 4

A copy of the British Library Cataloguing-in-Publication
Data is available from the British Library.

Printed and bound in the EC.

This independent publication has been prepared without any
involvement on the part of Liverpool Football Club or the
FA Premier League.

LIVERPOOL

PACKED WITH INFORMATION ON THE REDS

Hugh and Ian Westbrook

· PARRAGON ·

FACTFILE
LIVERPOOL

CONTENTS

INTRODUCTION

More than any other English club, Liverpool have been judged by the highest standards of consistency. Those standards were set under the late, great Bill Shankly and were continued under his successor, Bob Paisley – and every manager and team since, including Roy Evans' 1998 outfit, has been expected to live up to the excellence of their predecessors.

There's little doubting that the current side has individuals who deserve to be up there alongside Hunt, St John, Dalglish and Keegan. Michael Owen, the 18-year-old who forced his way into the national squad, the prolific Robbie Fowler, full-of-flair Steve McManaman, the exciting Jamie Redknapp – all these and more will doubtless keep the Anfield tradition alive.

That history, over a century of it, has been divided into easily digestible sections in the hope that it will inform and entertain you. It is not intended to be exhaustive, and anyone wanting more facts and figures would do well to obtain one of the weighty club histories available, or follow Liverpool's progress through the annual *Rothmans Football Yearbook*.

In these pages, however, you'll find details of the great players and double acts, profiles of the managers together with their achievements, quotes, statistics, dream teams…in short, much of what has gone to make the mighty Reds a footballing legend.

GOALS GALORE!

Liverpool's history is littered with great goalscorers, especially in the modern era with players like Kenny Dalglish, Kevin Keegan, John Toshack, Roger Hunt, Ian Rush and Robbie Fowler all donning the famous red shirt.

Welsh international Rush holds the club's all-time career goalscoring record after hitting 335 in his 15 seasons at Anfield. His most prolific campaign was 1983–84 when he plundered an astonishing 47 goals in all competitions to help Liverpool land three trophies. His 32 goals ensured the Reds would be League Champions for the 15th time, while eight more in the League Cup and five in the European Cup brought those trophies back to Anfield.

In all he scored 228 League goals for Liverpool after joining them from Chester and 107 in all other competitions. His total beat the previous record holder, England World Cup winner Roger Hunt, who claimed 285 goals in a Liverpool shirt.

No one at any club has scored more than Rush's record five goals in FA Cup Finals, while he has also hit more goals than anyone else in the League Cup: his total of 48 by the time he left Anfield eclipsed the record of former England star Geoff Hurst.

Rush, who also once notched four at Goodison Park, is one of four Liverpool players to hit five in a game. He achieved the feat in a 6-0 First Division win over Luton in 1983. The other five-goal stars were Andy McGuigan in the 7-0 defeat of Stoke in 1902, John Evans to help Liverpool beat Bristol Rovers 5-3 in 1954 and, most amazingly, 18 year-old Robbie Fowler in only his fourth start for the side in a 5-0 Coca-Cola Cup thrashing of Fulham in 1993.

Fulham had felt the Liverpool lash before, having also suffered a 10-0 hammering in the same competition seven years earlier – this the Reds' best League Cup win. In fact Liverpool have only scored more than ten in a match once in their history when they beat Norwegian part-timers Stromsgodset 11-0 in the Cup Winners' Cup in 1974. Nine different players got on the scoresheet that night with only goalkeeper Ray Clemence and midfielder Brian Hall missing out.

A similar thing happened in the 9-0 thrashing of Crystal Palace in a First Division match in 1989 with eight of the 13 Liverpool players who took part in the match beating Palace goalkeeper Perry Suckling. John Aldridge came on as a substitute that night and was allowed to take a penalty, which he scored, in his final Reds appearance before moving to Real Sociedad. Aldridge left however with the ignominious record of becoming the first player to miss a penalty in a Wembley

Cup Final after Dave Beasant denied him in the 1988 FA Cup.

Aldridge had enjoyed better fortune when he joined Liverpool the previous season, however, as he became one of a rare band of players who had scored on their full debut for the club. After an uneventful bow in a Liverpool shirt as a substitute at Aston Villa, he endeared himself to the Anfield faithful a week later by scoring the winner in his first full start against Southampton.

Kenny Dalglish was another to win instant acclaim from the Liverpool fans as he scored in each of his first three games following his British record move from Celtic in 1977. He was ever-present in his first three seasons at Anfield and leading scorer in the first two of them. Kevin Keegan also scored on his Liverpool debut, a 3-1 win over Nottingham Forest in August 1971.

Meanwhile Liverpool's biggest League win, a little before Keegan's time, was recorded last century when they beat Rotherham 10-1 in a Division Two match in 1896 with just four players sharing Liverpool's goals in the match. That result contributed to the side's biggest-ever haul in a season – 106 in just 30 games with five players scoring over ten goals each during the campaign.

Liverpool have always been good at stopping goals as well as scoring them. When they won the League Championship in 1979 they conceded just 16 in their 42 matches, still a League record, with Ray Clemence keeping 28 clean sheets.

Finally, Anfield's current scoring machine Michael Owen kept hitting the net everywhere apart from Anfield at the start of his career until he finally hit a hat-trick there against Grimsby in the Coca-Cola Cup in November 1997. There seems little doubt that he, along with Robbie Fowler and high-priced import Karlheinz Riedle, will find more chapters to add to the Anfield goals story in the future.

THROUGH THE YEARS
JANUARY

1994
January
28

Graeme Souness was sacked as Liverpool's manager after nearly three years in charge. Apart from an FA Cup triumph, Souness's reign had been unmemorable, with a high turnover of players, a fundamental change in the way the club had been successfully training and grooming its players and even the old bootroom had been knocked down so that a new press room could be built.

With the team not performing to expectations in the League and a shock FA Cup exit at home to First Division Bristol City to contend with, there was little surprise when Souness was replaced by Roy Evans.

1978
January

Ironically January was also the month when Souness the player had first arrived at the club as a £350,000 recruit from Middlesbrough in 1978. With Kenny Dalglish and Alan Hansen, he was to prove the backbone of a number of Liverpool's successes, making his acrimonious departure 16 years later all the more disappointing.

1959

January

15

Back in 1959, Liverpool suffered their most embarrassing FA Cup defeat, going down 2-1 at Worcester City. Billy Liddell was dropped for the game, making it the first FA Cup tie he had missed since the war.

1946

January

26

They also suffered their worst FA Cup defeat in January, Bolton beating them 5-0 in the first leg of the Fourth Round. Four days later, the Reds triumphed 2-0 in the home leg.

1990

January

9

In complete contrast, Liverpool's biggest ever win in the FA Cup was also recorded in January, when Swansea were beaten 8-0 in a Third Round replay after the first game had finished goalless at the Vetch Field. Ian Rush scored a hat-trick in the record scoreline.

DREAM TEAM 1

The Liverpool team which beat Newcastle to claim the 1974 FA Cup featured many of the players who had won the League and UEFA Cup in 1972-73, and formed the basis of the side which would gather further European glory towards the end of the decade as well as two more Championships.

Goalkeeper   **Ray Clemence**

Clemence had arrived from Scunthorpe in June 1967 and was Liverpool's regular keeper throughout the 1970s, as well as picking up more than 50 England caps. He collected five Championships as well as a host of European medals.

Right-back   **Tommy Smith**

Smith set up both Kevin Keegan's goals in the Cup Final victory against Newcastle. He was a tough defender with considerable skill, who featured in the club's 1965-66 Championship success and was still there when they won the European Cup 12 years later. Surprisingly he picked up just one England cap.

Central defender   **Phil Thompson**

Thompson was a Liverpool-born defender whose strength defied his spindly appearance. He was at Anfield until 1983 and captained the side for a time.

Central defender   **Emlyn Hughes**

The honour of lifting the 1974 FA Cup went to the irrepressible Emlyn Hughes. Captain of both club and country, Hughes was to lift two European Cups before he left Anfield, as well as winning two UEFA Cups and four Championships. His attitude and eagerness were an important driving force throughout the successes of the 1970s.

Left-back   **Alec Lindsay**

Lindsay was an attacking full-back who joined Liverpool from Bury in March 1969, leaving in August 1977. He played nearly 250 games for the club plus four England caps.

Midfielder   **Brian Hall**

Hall took some time to establish himself, but the energetic midfielder did enjoy some years in the 1970s when he was a regular, enabling him to pick up a Championship medal together with the FA Cup triumph.

Winger   **Ian Callaghan**

Callaghan was the only player to have been with Liverpool in the old Second Division who was to grace Wembley. The holder of the club's appearances record, his career culminated in the European Cup success in Rome.

Midfielder   **Peter Cormack**

Attacking Scottish international midfielder Cormack spent just over four years with Liverpool, having joined in July 1972 from Nottingham Forest. He played 168 times for the club and shared in the successes of the mid-1970s.

Striker   **Kevin Keegan**

England captain Keegan was the superstar of the line-up whose two goals inspired Liverpool to victory in the 1974 Final. His contribution to the club can never be overestimated.

Striker   **John Toshack**

Tall Welshman Toshack was picked ahead of Phil Boersma for the Cup Final, and it was fitting that his partnership with Keegan should celebrate Wembley success together.

Winger   **Steve Heighway**

Athletic winger Heighway completed the line-up: a highly skilled crosser of the ball, he was the first Liverpool player to be capped by the Republic of Ireland.

APPEARANCES

Liverpool's appearance record is held by Ian Callaghan. The only player to span the era from the Second Division to the European Cup, Callaghan made a total of 843 appearances, with five more as a substitute, of which 640 were League matches.

Callaghan started his career as an outside-right before moving into midfield and made his debut in April 1960 in the old Second Division against Bristol Rovers, leaving Anfield for Swansea City in September 1978. He played four matches for England over a 12-year period and was awarded an OBE.

Eight other players have made more than 500 appearances for the club. They are: Ray Clemence (656), Phil Neal (635), Tommy Smith (633), Ian Rush (643), Alan Hansen (607), Bruce Grobbelaar (579), Chris Lawler (546) and Billy Liddell (536).

In addition a further 13 players have played more than 400 times, including Kenny Dalglish, Roger Hunt, Emlyn Hughes, Ronnie Whelan, Phil Thompson, Ron Yeats, Steve Nicol and Ian St John.

Consistency of team selection has always been a Liverpool hallmark, and this is emphasised by the number of ever-presents they have had over the years. Left-back Duncan McLean didn't miss a match during the Reds' first two seasons as a League club, while left-half Willie Goldie didn't miss a game for three years from the 1900-01 season. Goldie also played a number of games in tandem with his brother Archie.

Apart from the early 1900s, it was rare for Liverpool to go for more than one season without at least one ever-present and between 1971-72 and 1986-87 no seasons were missed. However, Liverpool's lack of recent success can be highlighted by the fact that after 1989-90 it was not until 1994-95 that the Reds could once again boast of somebody not missing a game. In fact, there were two – David James and Robbie Fowler.

The biggest number of ever-presents was five, in the 1965-66 Championship season, when Gerry Byrne, Ian Callaghan, Tommy Lawrence, Tommy Smith and Ron Yeats appeared throughout. This impressive record has been equalled in 1968-69 and 1983-84, while on two further occasions there have been four ever-presents: 1961-62 when Liverpool won the Second Division Championship and the FA Cup winning season of 1973-74.

Those players with the most consistent runs include defender Phil Neal, who was ever-present for nine out of ten seasons from 1975-76, including eight consecutive campaigns; and goalkeepers Ray Clemence, four straight years from 1973-74;

and Bruce Grobbelaar, five years from 1981–82. One other notable ever-present from Liverpool's past was Manchester United legend Sir Matt Busby, who played right-half for Liverpool and didn't miss a match in 1938–39.

At the other end of the scale, a number of players have made just one appearance for the Reds. Some went on to forge successful careers elsewhere. Keith Burkinshaw made over 400 League appearances and then went into management with, among others, Tottenham and West Brom following his solitary bow for Liverpool in April 1955. Full-back Tom Lowry played his one game in April 1965 before going to Crewe where he established an appearance record for the club.

Two players made the most of their chance by scoring on their only appearance. Reserve forward B Bull netted Liverpool's second in a 6–1 victory over Lincoln City in January 1896, while inside-right John Sealey scored in Liverpool's 3–1 win at Wolves in April 1965.

Some odd coincidences have also been thrown up. A goalkeeper called Marshall made his only appearance in a Merseyside derby in January 1902, Liverpool losing 4–0 at Goodison Park. However, Harold McNaughton who did likewise in October 1920 enjoyed more luck than his predecessor as Liverpool won 1–0.

1967
February

Emlyn Hughes was signed from Blackpool for £65,000. Bill Shankly beat a host of other clubs to the signature of a man who would captain Liverpool to a string of trophies throughout the next 12 years.

1991
February
22

Kenny Dalglish announced that he was standing down as Liverpool's manager, adding that he was not going to wait for the end of the season. The strain of managing the club had finally got too much for him. His final game in charge was the 4-4 FA Cup draw at Everton, one of the most memorable Merseyside derbies of recent times. However, Liverpool had shown alarming defensive frailty during the match, possibly contributing to Dalglish's decision to leave. His reign had been highly successful, encompassing three Championships and two FA Cups, while Dalglish had also conducted himself with dignity during the recent Hillsborough tragedy.

1996
February
14

Dalglish's mentor Bob Paisley died in a Liverpool nursing home at the age of 77. His total of 19 trophies in nine seasons as manager will probably never be surpassed at the club.

GREAT STRIKERS

Liverpool have had many fine strikers and goalscoring partnerships. When the club became the major force that was to emerge under Bill Shankly, goals were obviously important in achieving his ambition of domestic domination and European excellence.

 ## ROGER HUNT

Roger Hunt first played for the club in the old Second Division when aged just 21, scoring in a 2-0 victory over Scunthorpe United in September 1959. He matched his age with 21 goals in his debut season of 1959-60. In the 1961-62 season he scored a club record 41 League goals as the Reds stormed to the Second Division Championship, scoring 99 goals in all. Hunt continued to score as Liverpool won the title in 1963-64, bagging 31 League goals, and when they won the title again 1965-66, Hunt scored the goals which clinched the title against Chelsea. He also notched the first goal in the club's 1965 FA Cup triumph.

Hunt played 34 times for England, including all six matches of the country's World Cup triumph. It was he who turned away to celebrate Geoff Hurst's crucial goal against West Germany in the Final when the ball came down off the bar, his reaction suggesting that the ball had crossed the line since he could easily have put the ball in to confirm the goal.

He left Liverpool for Bolton in December 1969 having played a total of 489 matches, scoring 285 goals, a record at the time. His strike rate of goals per game is nevertheless higher than Ian Rush, the man who was to break his record goal total. Roger Hunt retired in 1972 and that same year more than 56,000 paid tribute to him in a testimonial at Anfield.

ROGER HUNT LIVERPOOL RECORD 1959-69									
League		FA Cup		League Cup		Europe		Total	
Apps	Goals	Apps	Goals	Apps	Goals	Apps	Goals	Apps	Goals
404	245	44	18	10	5	31	17	489	285

 # KENNY DALGLISH

The goals in the first half of the 1970s were supplied largely by Kevin Keegan and John Toshack, and filling the void when Keegan went to Hamburg had seemed difficult. However, within a month of Keegan's departure, a record £440,000 had been spent on Celtic striker Kenny Dalglish. Although just 26, Dalglish had already scored 112 goals for Celtic in over 200 matches, won four Championships and four Scottish Cups, and represented Scotland 47 times.

Dalglish scored within seven minutes of his League debut at Middlesbrough and poached a further 28 as Liverpool finished second in the League. His 30th goal of the season came in the season's final match at Wembley, a delightful chip to beat Bruges and secure Liverpool's second European Cup.

Dalglish continued to grab the goals as Liverpool won five Championships, four League and three European Cups with him purely as a player. His 100th League goal for Liverpool had come in November 1983, making him the first player to score 100 goals in both the English and Scottish Leagues.

His ability was not just about goalscoring, he also possessed tremendous strength and was difficult to shake off the ball. Then there was the vision he showed when making goals, as Ian Rush would doubtless testify.

After the retirement of Joe Fagan and with the Heysel tragedy large in everyone's minds, Dalglish was appointed player-manager. He left himself out of the side early on, but returned and secured the title with the only goal of the last game of the season at Stamford Bridge. Liverpool won the Double and Dalglish was awarded Manager of the Year.

Dalglish finally stopped playing in 1989-90 and in total scored 168 goals from 481 starts. He took Liverpool to the title again in 1987-88 and 1989-90, looked after the club during the Hillsborough disaster, and then surprised everybody by resigning as manager in February 1991. He subsequently took over at Blackburn Rovers, steering them to the 1994-95 Premiership title, fittingly clinched at Anfield, and is currently in charge at Newcastle United.

KENNY DALGLISH LIVERPOOL RECORD 1977-90									
League		FA Cup		League Cup		Europe		Total	
Apps	Goals	Apps	Goals	Apps	Goals	Apps	Goals	Apps	Goals
355	118	36	13	59	27	47	10	457	168

IAN RUSH

When Ian Rush arrived at Anfield, he gave little indication of what he was to achieve. Signed from Chester for £300,000 in April 1980, the biggest fee ever paid at that time for a teenager, he played seven games in the 1980-81 season but failed to score. Advised by Bob Paisley to be more selfish, Rush returned with five goals in three games on his recall and 30 in all during 1981-82. He was leading scorer in every season bar one up to the 1986-87 season, twice notching at least 30 League goals and scoring 228 in all. His best season was 1983-84 when he managed 47 goals in all competitions.

With a whole host of clubs looking to sign him after his two goals had won the first all-Merseyside FA Cup Final for Liverpool, Rush opted to move to Italian giants Juventus – but even though the deal was sorted before the 1986-87 season, Rush was not due to move until after that campaign. That was also the season when the famous statistic of Liverpool never losing when Rush scored came to an end, Arsenal cancelling out his early goal to win the Littlewoods Cup Final. Rush's final home game, against Watford, was the predictable emotional affair, with Rush throwing his shirt into the Kop after scoring the only goal of the game, and he scored again in what was supposed to be his final game for the Reds at Chelsea.

Twelve months later, Rush was back. He hadn't settled in Italy and so he returned to continue his remarkable goalscoring. John Aldridge, signed as Rush's replacement, eventually had to make way. Rush came off the bench in the second FA Cup Final showdown with Everton, and once again struck twice to the secure the trophy.

Rush finally made his second emotional departure at the end of the 1995-96 having broken the all-time Liverpool scoring record. As well as his prolific finishing, Rush possessed a prodigious workrate and terrific speed.

His final tally was 335 goals in all competitions from 643 appearances. Everton were his favourite opponents, conceding 25 goals to him, a total which eclipsed Dixie Dean's long-held record for Merseyside encounters. He fired 16 hat-tricks and is the all-time top scorer in the FA Cup. Rush spent a disappointing season with Leeds and is now with former strike partner Kenny Dalglish at Newcastle.

IAN RUSH LIVERPOOL RECORD 1980-87, 1988-96									
League		FA Cup		League Cup		Europe		Total	
Apps	Goals	Apps	Goals	Apps	Goals	Apps	Goals	Apps	Goals
469	228	59	39	78	48	37	20	643	335

ROBBIE FOWLER

Former Everton fan Robbie Fowler emerged as the latest great Liverpool striker in emphatic fashion. Given his chance as an 18-year-old by Graeme Souness with Liverpool in the middle of a scoring drought, Fowler netted on his debut away to Fulham in the Coca-Cola Cup at Fulham in September 1993. The Reds won the game 3-1 and triumphed 5-0 in the return, Fowler scoring all five to announce his arrival. His first League goal came against Oldham and he scored 18 times in all in the 1993-94 season. He started the following season in grand style, a high-speed hat-trick notched within five minutes putting paid to Arsenal at Anfield. Fowler totalled an impressive 31 goals for the season and also picked up a Coca-Cola Cup winner's medal.

The signing of Stan Collymore for the following season saw Fowler temporarily relegated to the substitute's bench. However, Collymore was injured shortly after the start of the season, and Robbie reclaimed his place to register 36 goals during the campaign, including another Anfield hat-trick against Arsenal. His form saw him included in the England squad for Euro '96, where he made four appearances as substitute.

Fowler kept up his prolific strike rate with another 31 goals in the 1996-97 campaign, including his first for England in a friendly with Mexico. His 100th goal for Liverpool was the second of the four he managed against Middlesbrough in

December, reaching the milestone in one fewer game than it had taken Ian Rush. He also showed his sporting nature in a game at Arsenal when protesting that opposing keeper David Seaman had not touched him when the referee awarded a penalty. Fowler was voted PFA Young Player of the Year in both 1994–95 and the following season.

ROBBIE FOWLER LIVERPOOL RECORD 1993–(97)									
League		FA Cup		League Cup		Europe		Total	
Apps	Goals	Apps	Goals	Apps	Goals	Apps	Goals	Apps	Goals
140	83	16	9	21	17	11	7	188	116

BEST SEASON 1

Having won 18 Championships (to 1997) and a whole host of other trophies, Liverpool have had many memorable seasons. However, the 1976–77 was unforgettable for a whole host of reasons.

L iverpool began their League campaign with just two defeats in their first 16 games to sit on top of the table, including putting five goals past old foes Leicester City. They then lost twice in a week, the first a 5-1 mauling at Aston Villa, which was the first time they had conceded more than four goals in the whole of the 1970s. However, they picked themselves up to beat Stoke City 4-0, going on to take the title with an amazing run of 11 undefeated games. The title was clinched on 14 May with a goalless draw at home to West Ham. Kevin Keegan and John Toshack predictably led the goalscoring charts, notching 22 League goals between them, while 11 other players got on the scoresheet.

Liverpool's trophy assault was also running through two other competitions. Having beaten Crystal Palace, Carlisle United, Oldham Athletic and Middlesbrough to reach the Semi-Finals of the FA Cup, Liverpool faced neighbours Everton for the fourth time at that stage of the competition. The first encounter finished 2-2, but Liverpool comfortably won the second game 3-0.

The Reds' attempt to achieve the domestic Double came unstuck at Wembley when they faced a Manchester United side determined to overcome their own surprise defeat in the Final the year before. Stuart Pearson put United ahead early in the second half, Jimmy Case struck a memorable equaliser a couple of minutes later, but within three minutes United had scored the winner through Jimmy Greenhoff after a goalmouth scramble.

This was not the end of Liverpool's season, though – far from it. They now had to go to Rome for their first ever European Cup Final and forget the disappointment of Wembley. They had reached the Final with victories over Crusaders, Trabsonzpor, memorably against St Etienne and Zurich. They were not to be denied and, with more than 30,000 fans cheering them on, Terry McDermott, Tommy Smith and Phil Neal (from the penalty spot) capped a memorable performance as Liverpool lifted the trophy for the first time.

1976-77 LEAGUE RECORD

Opponents	Home	Away
Arsenal	2-0	1-1
Aston Villa	3-0	1-5
Birmingham City	4-1	1-2
Bristol City	2-1	1-2
Coventry City	3-1	0-0
Derby County	3-1	3-2
Everton	3-1	0-0
Ipswich Town	2-1	0-1
Leeds United	3-1	1-1
Leicester City	5-1	1-0
Manchester City	2-1	1-1
Manchester United	1-0	0-0
Middlesbrough	0-0	1-0
Newcastle United	1-0	0-1
Norwich City	1-0	1-2
Queens Park Rangers	3-1	1-1
Stoke City	4-0	0-0
Sunderland	2-0	1-0
Tottenham Hotspur	2-0	0-1
West Bromwich Albion	1-1	1-0
West Ham United	0-0	0-2

DERBY  FOCUS

Despite their intense rivalry, clashes between Liverpool and Everton have always been noted for their sporting nature and the camaraderie in the crowd. This could be due to how closely intertwined the histories of the two clubs are.

Everton played their first game on 23 December 1879 and joined the Lancashire Association the following year. Games were played on the public pitch at Liverpool's Stanley Park. However, a ruling in 1882 forced the club to look for an enclosed ground, and they eventually moved into Anfield in 1884. Substantial sums were invested by local businessman John Houlding in improving the ground but, following disagreements with John Orrell, from whom Anfield was rented, there was a split in the Everton hierarchy and the club decided to leave Anfield, buying the site of Goodison Park. Anfield was left empty and Houlding decided to fill it by creating a new club – so Liverpool FC was born.

When Houlding died in 1902, flags at both grounds flew at half-mast and the pall-bearers were players from both clubs. The first League match between Liverpool and Everton took place at Goodison on 13 October 1893 in Liverpool's debut season in the First Division, and 44,000 saw Everton triumph 3-0. The return match a month later finished 2-2, with 30,000 watching the game. Liverpool were relegated that season, but returned 12 months later and in the following season finished fifth to become the city's top club for the first time.

Up to the end of the 1996-97 campaign (as detailed in the table below), Liverpool and Everton had contested 156 League matches, all of which have been in England's top division. Indeed, when Everton were last in the old Second Division, they were promoted in 1953-54 and passed Liverpool who were on the way down! Liverpool have the better overall record with 56 victories. Everton's 54th win came in the 157th League meeting early in the 1997-98 season. Liverpool have scored 211 goals to Everton's 195. Eleven encounters have been in the Premiership, with Everton winning five and Liverpool just two.

Competition	P	W	D	L	F	A
Football League	156	56	47	53	210	193
FA Cup	20	9	5	6	34	24
League Cup	4	2	1	1	2	1
Charity Shield	3	1	1	1	2	2
War games	51	26	9	16	111	97
Total	**234**	**94**	**63**	**77**	**359**	**317**

Liverpool have registered a number of big wins over Everton in League encounters. In 1922-23, the year of the Reds' fourth League title, Everton were beaten 5-1 at Anfield. In 1932-33 Harold Barton grabbed a hat-trick in the Reds' 7-4 triumph, and three years later the Anfield margin was 6-0. In 1982-83 Ian Rush scored four times in Liverpool's 5-0 victory at Goodison.

The 1980s were a period of Merseyside dominance in English football. If Liverpool weren't Champions, then it seemed their neighbours were. Everton recorded their first victory at Anfield for 15 years on their way to the title in 1984-85 – but, despite repeating the win the following season to establish a big lead at the top of the table, Liverpool's storming finish saw them pass their rivals to claim the prize.

In 1986-87 Everton visited Anfield knowing that a win would all but clinch the Championship for them. Liverpool won 3-1, but couldn't prevent Everton from finishing top. The season after that it was Liverpool's turn, as the Reds looked to go the whole season without losing. Liverpool equalled Leeds United's record of 29 unbeaten matches from the start of the season, but came unstuck in the 30th, losing 1-0 at Goodison. The following season Arsenal won the title at Liverpool's expense, stopping the years of Merseyside victories. The season was dominated by the Hillsborough tragedy, and after their period of mourning, Liverpool's first match fittingly took place at Goodison, finishing 0-0.

Liverpool and Everton have also shared many memorable Cup encounters. Their first FA Cup meeting was in 1901-02, Liverpool triumphing 2-0 after a First Round replay. Everton put Liverpool out in the First Round three years later. The following season, 1905-06, the pair reached the Semi-Finals and were drawn together. The game was played at Villa Park and 50,000 made their way down from Liverpool to see Everton win 2-0. Everton went on to lift the Cup while Liverpool won the League.

Everton and Liverpool met twice more, in 1910-11 and 1931-32, each side emerging victorious once before the Reds took their Semi-Final revenge in 1949-50, winning 2-0 in front of 73,000 at Maine Road. Future manager Bob Paisley scored the first, but was dropped for the Final, which Liverpool lost 2-0 to Arsenal.

Liverpool's only solace in their first season back in the Second Division in 1954-55 was a 4-0 Fourth Round FA Cup victory at Goodison. It came during a period when the two had no League clashes, from January 1951 to September 1962, as they were in separate divisions. Everton triumphed 1-0 in the Fifth Round of the 1966-67 competition, with the game being shown live on a giant television screen at Anfield. The next meeting was a Semi-Final in 1970-71, Liverpool coming from behind to win 2-1. However, like the last time they beat Everton in the Semi-Final, the Final brought Arsenal and defeat. There was another Semi-Final in 1976-77, Liverpool winning 3-0 at Maine Road following a 2-2 draw. Again they lost the Final, this time to Manchester United.

Finally a Semi-Final draw was to keep the clubs apart, and while Liverpool were beating Southampton 2-0 in 1985-86, Everton beat Sheffield Wednesday to set up an all-Merseyside Final after 93 years of trying. The encounter saw Everton dominate the first-half to lead through Gary Lineker, but two second-half goals from Ian Rush and one for Craig Johnston secured the Cup and the Double for Liverpool.

Two years later Liverpool beat Everton 1-0 at Goodison on the way to the Final, and the following season, 1988-89, saw the Merseyside giants back at Wembley for the second all-Merseyside Final. The game was played in the shadow of the Hillsborough disaster. John Aldridge's early goal looked to have won the Cup for the Reds, but Stuart McCall's late equaliser forced extra-time. Two goals from substitute Ian Rush saw Liverpool victorious, McCall scoring again for Everton.

The most recent FA Cup meeting between the clubs is perhaps the most memorable of all. Drawn together in the Fifth Round of the 1990-91 competition, a goalless draw at Anfield was followed by an epic 4-4 encounter at Goodison. Four times Liverpool led through two goals from Peter Beardsley and one each for Ian Rush and John Barnes, and four times Everton equalised, two goals each by Graeme Sharp and Tony Cottee.

Afterwards manager Kenny Dalglish described it as the best Cup-tie he'd ever seen. However, admiration for the excitement of the match did not disguise the pressure he was feeling, and within 48 hours his resignation from the manager's job was confirmed.

Liverpool and Everton's first clash in the League Cup was in the Final of the 1983-84 competition, the first ever meeting of the two clubs at Wembley. The good feeling between them was again emphasised by the chants of 'Merseyside,

Merseyside' which were heard after the sides had played out a goalless draw. Graeme Souness scored the goal which won the Maine Road replay for the Reds. There have been two further games in the League Cup, with each side claiming one 1-0 victory. Many players have played across both sides of Stanley Park. Peter Beardsley and Gary Ablett both made the move to Everton from Liverpool in the 1990s, while midfielder Steve McMahon started his career with Everton and joined Liverpool from Aston Villa. Meanwhile Kevin Sheedy, who was a regular for Everton during their successes of the 1980s, made his League debut for Liverpool.

There is one other notable thing that Liverpool and Everton shared. For nearly 50 years, until 1934, the production of Liverpool and Everton's matchday programme was shared, and came out each week with details of the first-team game being played in the city as well as the reserve match taking place at the neighbour's ground.

LIVERPOOL'S TOP 10 DERBY APPEARANCES			
1	Ian Rush	1980-87, 1988-96	36
2	Bruce Grobbelaar	1981-94	33
3	Alan Hansen	1977-90	32
4	Ian Callaghan	1959-78	31
5=	Phil Neal	1974-86	29
5=	Ronnie Whelan	1980-94	29
7=	Ray Clemence	1968-81	27
7=	Tommy Smith	1962-78	27
9	Emlyn Hughes	1966-79	26
10=	Arthur Goddard	1901-14	25
10=	Steve Nicol	1981-94	25

THROUGH THE YEARS
MARCH

1936
March
22

John McKenna died. An Irish businessman, he was the club's first ever manager, and his determination helped the club to recover from its instant relegation from the First Division by going straight back up and claiming their first Championship not long after.

1981
March

Bruce Grobbelaar joined Liverpool from Vancouver Whitecaps. When Ray Clemence left the club a few months later, the unconventional Grobbelaar was thrust into the limelight and became one of Liverpool's most decorated keepers.

1990
March
31

Flying Israeli winger Ronnie Rosenthal made his debut on loan for Liverpool against Southampton in March 1990, and it was his performances which helped propel the Reds to their 18th and most recent Championship.

1982
March
13

Liverpool won the second of four consecutive League Cups despite coming up against Ray Clemence, who had left them during the previous close-season, in goal for Tottenham Hotspur. Spurs led 1-0 through Steve Archibald until, with just two minutes remaining, Ronnie Whelan struck the equaliser. Whelan (again) and Ian Rush claimed the trophy in extra-time.

1983
March
26

Manchester United led the League (Milk) Cup Final 1-0 through Norman Whiteside, but Alan Kennedy produced another of his famous goals to equalise and Ronnie Whelan's curler won it in extra-time. This allowed Bob Paisley – in his last season as boss – to be given the honour of climbing the stairs at Wembley to become the first manager to collect a trophy at the stadium.

1984
March
25

Liverpool and Everton met for the first time at Wembley but, despite the unique atmosphere, neither side could score. They met again three days later at Maine Road and Graeme Souness struck the only goal to give Liverpool the League Cup for the fourth time.

FA CUP RECORD

Liverpool's first FA Cup campaign pre–dated their League membership. So far, they've taken the country's premier knockout trophy five times.

Stage	Opponents	Score
1892-93		
Qualifier 1	Nantwich	4-0
Qualifier 2	Newtown	9-0
Qualifier 3	Northwich Vic	1-2
1893-94		
Round 1	Grimsby T	3-0
Round 2	Preston NE	3-2
Round 3	Bolton W	0-3
1894-95		
Round 1	Barnsley St Peters	2-1, 4-0
Following a Barnsley protest the first match was declared a draw		
Round 2	Nott'm Forest	0-2
1895-96		
Round 1	Millwall	4-1
Round 2	Wolves	0-2
1896-97		
Round 1	Burton Swifts	4-3
Round 2	West Brom	2-1
Round 3	Nott'm Forest	1-1, 1-0
Semi-Final	Aston Villa	0-3

Stage	Opponents	Score
1897-98		
Round 1	Hucknall St J	2-0
Round 2	Newton Heath	0-0, 2-1
Round 3	Derby Co	1-1, 1-5
1898-99		
Round 1	Blackburn R	2-0
Round 2	Newcastle Utd	3-1
Round 3	West Brom	2-0
Semi-Final	Sheffield Utd	2-2, 4-4, 1-0*, 0-1

Match Abandoned

Stage	Opponents	Score
1899-1900		
Round 1	Stoke	0-0, 1-0
Round 2	West Brom	1-1, 1-2
1900-01		
Round 1	Notts Co	0-2
1901-02		
Round 1	Everton	2-2, 2-0
Round 2	Southampton	1-4
1902-03		
Round 1	Manchester Utd	1-2
1903-04		
Round 1	Blackburn R	1-3
1904-05		
Round 1	Everton	1-1, 1-2

LIVERPOOL

Stage	Opponents	Score
1905-06		
Round 1	Leicester Fosse	2-1
Round 2	Barnsley	1-0
Round 3	Brentford	2-0
Round 4	Southampton	3-0
Semi-Final	Everton	0-2
1906-07		
Round 1	Birmingham	2-1
Round 2	Oldham Ath	1-0
Round 3	Bradford C	1-0
Round 4	Sheffield Wed	0-1
1907-08		
Round 1	Derby Co	4-2
Round 2	Brighton & HA	1-1, 3-0
Round 3	Newcastle Utd	1-3
1908-09		
Round 1	Lincoln C	5-1
Round 2	Norwich C	2-3
1909-10		
Round 1	Bristol C	0-2
1910-11		
Round 1	Gainsborough T	3-2
Round 2	Everton	1-2
1911-12		
Round 1	Leyton	1-0
Round 2	Fulham	0-3

Stage	Opponents	Score
1912-13		
Round 1	Bristol C	3-0
Round 2	Woolwich Arsenal	4-1
Round 3	Newcastle Utd	1-1, 0-1
1913-14		
Round 1	Barnsley	1-1, 1-0
Round 2	Gillingham	2-0
Round 3	West Ham Utd	1-1, 5-1
Round 4	QPR	2-1
Semi-Final	Aston Villa	2-0
Final	Burnley	0-1
1914-15		
Round 1	Stockport Co	3-0
Round 2	Sheffield Utd	0-1
1919-20		
Round 1	South Shields	1-1, 2-0
Round 2	Luton T	2-0
Round 3	Birmingham	2-0
Round 4	Huddersfield T	1-2
1920-21		
Round 1	Manchester Utd	1-1, 2-1
Round 2	Newcastle Utd	0-1
1921-22		
Round 1	Sunderland	1-1, 5-0
Round 2	West Brom	0-1

Stage	Opponents	Score
1922-23		
Round 1	Arsenal	0-0, 4-1
Round 2	Wolves	2-0
Round 3	Sheffield Utd	1-2
1923-24		
Round 1	Bradford C	2-1
Round 2	Bolton W	4-1
Round 3	Southampton	0-0, 2-0
Round 4	Newcastle Utd	0-1
1924-25		
Round 1	Leeds Utd	3-0
Round 2	Bristol C	1-0
Round 3	Birmingham	2-1
Round 4	Southampton	0-1
1925-26		
Round 3	Southampton	0-0, 1-0
Round 4	Fulham	1-3
1926-27		
Round 3	Bournemouth	1-1, 4-1
Round 4	Southport	3-1
Round 5	Arsenal	0-2
1927-28		
Round 3	Darlington	1-0
Round 4	Cardiff C	1-2
1928-29		
Round 3	Bristol C	2-0
Round 4	Bolton W	0-0, 2-5

Stage	Opponents	Score
1929-30		
Round 3	Cardiff C	1-2
1930-31		
Round 3	Birmingham	0-2
1931-32		
Round 3	Everton	2-1
Round 4	Chesterfield	4-2
Round 5	Grimsby T	1-0
Round 6	Chelsea	0-2
1932-33		
Round 3	West Brom	0-2
1933-34		
Round 3	Fulham	1-1, 3-2
Round 4	Tranmere R	3-1
Round 5	Bolton W	0-3
1934-35		
Round 3	Yeovil & Petters Utd	6-2
Round 4	Blackburn R	0-1
1935-36		
Round 3	Swansea T	1-0
Round 4	Arsenal	0-2
1936-37		
Round 3	Norwich C	0-3

Stage	Opponents	Score
1937-38		
Round 3	Crystal Palace	0-0, 3-1
Round 4	Sheffield Utd	1-1, 1-0
Round 5	Huddersfield T	0-1
1938-39		
Round 3	Luton T	3-0
Round 4	Stockport Co	5-1
Round 5	Wolves	1-4
1945-46		
Round 3	Chester	2-0, 2-1
Round 4	Bolton W	0-5, 2-0
1946-47		
Round 3	Walsall	5-2
Round 4	Grimsby T	2-0
Round 5	Derby Co	1-0
Round 6	Birmingham C	4-1
Semi-Final	Burnley	0-0, 0-1
1947-48		
Round 3	Nott'm Forest	4-1
Round 4	Manchester Utd	0-3
1948-49		
Round 3	Nott'm Forest	2-2, 4-0
Round 4	Notts Co	1-0
Round 5	Wolves	1-3
1949-50		
Round 3	Blackburn R	0-0, 2-1
Round 4	Exeter C	3-1

Stage	Opponents	Score
Round 5	Stockport Co	2-1
Round 6	Blackpool	2-1
Semi-Final	Everton	2-0
Final	Arsenal	0-2

1950-51

Round 3	Norwich C	1-3

1951-52

Round 3	Workington	1-0
Round 4	Wolves	2-1
Round 5	Burnley	0-2

1952-53

Round 3	Gateshead	0-1

1953-54

Round 3	Bolton W	0-1

1954-55

Round 3	Lincoln C	1-1, 1-0
Round 4	Everton	4-0
Round 5	Huddersfield T	0-2

1955-56

Round 3	Accrington S	2-0
Round 4	Scunthorpe Utd	3-3, 2-1
Round 5	Manchester C	0-0, 1-2

1956-57

Round 3	Southend Utd	1-2

Stage	Opponents	Score
1957-58		
Round 3	Southend Utd	1-1, 3-2
Round 4	Northampton T	3-1
Round 5	Scunthorpe Utd	1-0
Round 6	Blackburn R	1-2
1958-59		
Round 3	Worcester C	1-2
1959-60		
Round 3	Leyton Orient	2-1
Round 4	Manchester Utd	1-3
1960-61		
Round 3	Coventry C	3-2
Round 4	Sunderland	0-2
1961-62		
Round 3	Chelsea	4-3
Round 4	Oldham Ath	2-1
Round 5	Preston NE	0-0, 0-0, 0-1
1962-63		
Round 3	Wrexham	3-0
Round 4	Burnley	1-1, 2-1
Round 5	Arsenal	2-1
Round 6	West Ham Utd	1-0
Semi-Final	Leicester C	0-1
1963-64		
Round 3	Derby Co	5-0
Round 4	Port Vale	0-0, 2-1
Round 5	Arsenal	1-0
Round 6	Swansea T	1-2

Stage	Opponents	Score
1964-65		
Round 3	West Brom	2-1
Round 4	Stockport Co	1-1, 2-0
Round 5	Bolton W	1-0
Round 6	Leicester C	0-0, 1-0
Semi-Final	Chelsea	2-0
Final	Leeds Utd	2-1
1965-66		
Round 3	Chelsea	1-2
1966-67		
Round 3	Watford	0-0, 3-1
Round 4	Aston Villa	1-0
Round 5	Everton	0-1
1967-68		
Round 3	Bournemouth	0-0, 4-1
Round 4	Walsall	0-0, 5-2
Round 5	Tottenham H	1-1, 2-1
Round 6	West Brom	0-0, 1-1, 1-2
1968-69		
Round 3	Doncaster R	2-0
Round 4	Burnley	2-1
Round 5	Leicester C	0-0, 0-1
1969-70		
Round 3	Coventry C	1-1, 3-0
Round 4	Wrexham	3-1
Round 5	Leicester C	0-0, 2-0
Round 6	Watford	0-1

Stage	Opponents	Score
	1970-71	
Round 3	Aldershot	1-0
Round 4	Swansea C	3-0
Round 5	Southampton	1-0
Round 6	Tottenham H	0-0, 1-0
Semi-Final	Everton	2-1
Final	Arsenal	1-2
	1971-72	
Round 3	Oxford Utd	3-0
Round 4	Leeds Utd	0-0, 0-2
	1972-73	
Round 3	Burnley	0-0, 3-0
Round 4	Manchester C	0-0, 0-2
	1973-74	
Round 3	Doncaster R	2-2, 2-0
Round 4	Carlisle Utd	0-0, 2-0
Round 5	Ipswich T	2-0
Round 6	Bristol C	1-0
Semi-Final	Leicester C	0-0, 3-1
Final	Newcastle Utd	3-0
	1974-75	
Round 3	Stoke C	2-0
Round 4	Ipswich T	0-1
	1975-76	
Round 3	West Ham Utd	2-0
Round 4	Derby Co	0-1

FACTFILE
LIVERPOOL

Stage	Opponents	Score
1976-77		
Round 3	Crystal Palace	0-0, 3-2
Round 4	Carlisle Utd	3-0
Round 5	Oldham Ath	3-1
Round 6	Middlesbrough	2-0
Semi-Final	Everton	2-2, 3-0
Final	Manchester Utd	1-2
1977-78		
Round 3	Chelsea	2-4
1978-79		
Round 3	Southend Utd	0-0, 3-0
Round 4	Blackburn R	1-0
Round 5	Burnley	1-0
Round 6	Ipswich T	1-0
Semi-Final	Manchester Utd	2-2, 0-1
1979-80		
Round 3	Grimsby T	5-0
Round 4	Nott'm Forest	2-0
Round 5	Bury	2-0
Round 6	Tottenham H	1-0
Semi-Final	Arsenal	0-0, 1-1, 1-1, 0-1
1980-81		
Round 3	Altrincham	4-1
Round 4	Everton	1-2
1981-82		
Round 3	Swansea C	4-0
Round 4	Sunderland	3-0
Round 5	Chelsea	0-2

Stage	Opponents	Score
1982-83		
Round 3	Blackburn R	2-1
Round 4	Stoke C	2-0
Round 5	Brighton & HA	1-2
1983-84		
Round 3	Newcastle Utd	4-0
Round 4	Brighton & HA	0-2
1984-85		
Round 3	Aston Villa	3-0
Round 4	Tottenham H	1-0
Round 5	York C	1-1, 7-0
Round 6	Barnsley	4-0
Semi-Final	Manchester Utd	2-2, 1-2
1985-86		
Round 3	Norwich C	5-0
Round 4	Chelsea	2-1
Round 5	York C	1-1, 3-1
Round 6	Watford	0-0, 2-1
Semi-Final	Southampton	2-0
Final	Everton	3-1
1986-87		
Round 3	Luton T	0-0, 0-0, 0-3
1987-88		
Round 3	Stoke C	0-0, 1-0
Round 4	Aston Villa	2-0
Round 5	Everton	1-0
Round 6	Manchester C	4-0
Semi-Final	Nott'm Forest	2-1
Final	Wimbledon	0-1

Stage	Opponents	Score
1988-89		
Round 3	Carlisle Utd	3-0
Round 4	Millwall	2-0
Round 5	Hull C	3-2
Round 6	Brentford	4-0
Semi-Final	Nott'm Forest	0-0*, 3-1
* Hillsborough Semi-Final abandoned after six minutes		
Final	Everton	3-2
1989-90		
Round 3	Swansea C	0-0, 8-0
Round 4	Norwich C	0-0, 3-1
Round 5	Southampton	3-0
Round 6	QPR	2-2, 1-0
Semi-Final	Crystal Palace	3-4
1990-91		
Round 3	Blackburn R	1-1, 3-0
Round 4	Brighton & HA	2-2, 3-2
Round 5	Everton	0-0, 4-4, 0-1
1991-92		
Round 3	Crewe Alex	4-0
Round 4	Bristol R	1-1, 2-1
Round 5	Ipswich T	0-0, 3-2
Round 6	Aston Villa	1-0
Semi-Final	Portsmouth	1-1, 0-0 (3-2 pens)
Final	Sunderland	2-0
1992-93		
Round 3	Bolton W	2-2, 0-2

LIVERPOOL

Stage	Opponents	Score
1993-94		
Round 3	Bristol C	1-1*, 1-1, 0-1
	* Match abandoned	
1994-95		
Round 3	Birmingham C	0-0, 1-1 (2-0 pens)
Round 4	Burnley	0-0, 1-0
Round 5	Wimbledon	1-1, 2-0
Round 6	Tottenham H	1-2
1995-96		
Round 3	Rochdale	7-0
Round 4	Shrewsbury T	4-0
Round 5	Charlton Ath	2-1
Round 6	Leeds Utd	0-0, 3-0
Semi-Final	Aston Villa	3-0
Final	Manchester Utd	0-1
1996-97		
Round 3	Burnley	1-0
Round 4	Chelsea	2-4
1997-98		
Round 3	Coventry C	1-3

FA Cup Record Club By Club

Opposition	P	W	D	L	F-A
Accrington S	1	1	—	—	2-0
Aldershot	1	1	—	—	1-0
Altrincham	1	1	—	—	4-1
Arsenal	13	4	4	5	14-14
Aston Villa	7	6	—	1	12-3
Barnsley	4	3	1	—	7-1
Birmingham C	7	4	2	1	11-6
Blackburn R	10	5	2	3	13-9
Blackpool	1	1	—	—	2-1
Bolton W	11	3	2	6	11-22
Bournemouth	4	2	2	—	9-3
Bradford C	2	2	—	—	3-1
Brentford	2	2	—	—	6-0
Brighton & HA	6	2	2	2	10-9
Bristol C	7	4	1	2	8-4
Bristol R	2	1	1	—	3-2
Burnley	13	6	4	3	11-7
Burton Swifts	1	1	—	—	4-3
Bury	1	1	—	—	2-0
Cardiff C	2	—	—	2	2-4
Carlisle Utd	4	3	1	—	8-0
Charlton Ath	1	1	—	—	2-1
Chelsea	7	2	—	5	11-17
Chester	2	2	—	—	4-1
Chesterfield	1	1	—	—	4-2
Coventry C	4	2	1	1	8-6
Crewe Alex	1	1	—	—	4-0
Crystal Pal	5	2	2	1	9-7
Darlington	1	1	—	—	1-0
Derby Co	6	3	1	2	12-10
Doncaster R	3	2	1	—	6-2
Everton	20	9	5	6	34-25
Exeter C	1	1	—	—	3-1
Fulham	4	1	1	2	5-9
Gainsborough T	1	1	—	—	3-2
Gateshead	1	—	—	1	0-1
Gillingham	1	1	—	—	2-0
Grimsby T	4	4	—	—	10-0
Hucknall St J	1	1	—	—	2-0
Huddersfield T	3	—	—	3	1-5
Hull C	1	1	—	—	3-2
Ipswich T	5	3	1	1	6-3
Leicester C	9	3	4	2	8-4
Leeds United	6	3	2	1	8-3
Leyton Orient	2	2	—	—	3-1
Lincoln C	3	2	1	—	7-2
Luton T	5	2	2	1	5-3
Millwall	2	2	—	—	6-1
Nantwich	1	1	—	—	4-0
Manchester C	5	1	2	2	5-4
Man Utd	10	2	3	5	10-14
Middlesbrough	1	1	—	—	2-0
Newcastle Utd	7	2	1	4	9-7
Newtown	1	1	—	—	9-0
Northampton T	1	1	—	—	3-1
Northwich Vic	1	—	—	1	1-2
Norwich C	5	1	1	3	6-10
Nott'm Forest	8	5	2	1	15-7
Notts County	2	1	—	1	1-2
Oldham Ath	3	3	—	—	6-2
Oxford Utd	1	1	—	—	3-0
Port Vale	2	1	1	—	2-1
Portsmouth	2	—	2	—	1-1
Preston NE	4	1	2	1	3-3
QPR	3	2	1	—	5-3
Rochdale	1	1	—	—	7-0
Scunthorpe Utd	3	2	1	—	6-4
Sheffield Utd	7	1	3	3	9-11
Sheffield Wed	1	—	—	1	0-1
Shrewsbury T	1	1	—	—	4-0
South Shields	2	1	1	—	3-1
Southend Utd	5	2	2	1	8-5
Southampton	10	6	2	2	13-5
Southport	1	1	—	—	3-1
Stockport Co	5	4	1	—	13-3
Stoke C	6	4	2	—	6-0
Sunderland	5	3	1	1	11-3
Swansea C	6	4	1	1	17-2
Tottenham H	7	4	2	1	7-3
Tranmere R	1	1	—	—	3-1
Walsall	3	2	1	—	10-4
Watford	5	2	2	1	5-3
West Brom	10	3	3	4	10-11
West Ham Utd	4	3	1	—	9-2
Wimbledon	3	1	1	1	3-2
Wolves	5	2	—	3	6-10
Worcester C	1	—	—	1	1-2
Workington	1	1	—	—	1-0
Wrexham	2	2	—	—	6-1
Yeovil & P Utd	1	1	—	—	6-2
York C	2	1	1	—	4-2

CREAM OF THE CONTINENT

Liverpool have always been strongly represented by players from outside the region. Indeed, the original Liverpool squad was recruited from Scotland, and the entire team which contested the Reds' first League match came from north of the border. Subsequently players from all round the globe have played for Liverpool, a high number between the wars hailing from South Africa.

The influx started in 1925 following a tour to England by the South African amateur side. Goalkeeper Arthur Riley stayed behind to sign for the club, becoming the first of four South African-born keepers to play for Liverpool. He made 338 appearances and returned home in 1940. He was followed to Liverpool by striker Gordon Hodgson, who scored 240 goals in 378 League and Cup games, including a record 36 strikes in 1930–31, a figure later topped by Roger Hunt.

Hodgson also played cricket for Lancashire between 1928 and 1933. He eventually went into management and died while boss of Port Vale in 1951. Left-back Jimmy Gray was the third member of the touring party to be recruited, but he managed just one start for the Reds.

The 1930s imports included winger Berry Nieuwenhuys, known as Nivvy, who stayed until 1947, playing 260 games and scoring 79 goals, goalkeeper Dirk Kemp and outside-left Harman van den Berg. Winger Bob Priday played just after the war, while the 1950s brought 66 games for keeper Doug Rudham and six for inside-forward Hugh Gerhardi.

Liverpool's more recent South African-born recruits have tended to be associated with the countries they were raised in. Goalkeeper Bruce Grobbelaar played international football for Zimbabwe despite being born in South Africa, while Craig Johnston was born in South Africa of English and Welsh parentage and came to England from Australia. He returned down under in 1988 having scored in Liverpool's FA Cup triumph against Everton in 1986, one of 39 goals in 259 appearances. He later became known for designing the Predator football boot.

Aside from Europe, the furthest afield other Liverpool recruits have come from has been Israel. Defender Avi Cohen started just 16 League games between September 1979 and November 1981 due to the strength of Liverpool's defence. However, he did score when the Reds beat Aston Villa 4–1 to claim the 1979–80 title – though he owed Liverpool a goal having put through his own net to give Villa the lead! Ronnie Rosenthal arrived in March 1990 and helped to inspire Liverpool to their most recent title, scoring a hat-trick in his second full match against Charlton Athletic and seven in all that season. However, he never held down a regular place and left for Tottenham in January 1994. In 1997–98 he was inspiring Watford's Second Division promotion push.

A number of players have come from Scandinavia. Danish midfielder Jan Molby was signed for the 1984–85 season and made 251 appearances, despite a three-month spell in jail following a motoring conviction at the end of 1988.

Ex-Fiorentina defender Glenn Hysen quickly established himself in the side from August 1989. However, one of Graeme Souness's first acts as manager was to drop him, and he returned to his native Sweden shortly afterwards.

Norwegian defender Stig-Inge Bjornebye came from Rosenborg in December 1992 and eventually established himself in the side, despite at one stage returning to Rosenborg on loan. Denmark's Torben Piechnik arrived just before him, but stayed at the club for less than two years. Bjornebye was joined in January 1997 by former Rosenborg colleague Bjorn Tore Kvarme.

Danish goalkeeper Michael Stensgaard was Roy Evans' first purchase in July 1994 from Hvidovre, but he was forced to retire through injury two years later without having played a first-team game.

Another Danish keeper, Jorgen Nielsen, was signed in March 1997. Norwegian midfielder Oyvind Leonhardsen joined before the 1997–98 season for £3.5 million from Wimbledon.

There have been three other acquisitions from Europe. Hungarian defender Istvan Kozma was signed from Dunfermline in January 1992, but made only three full appearances before leaving the following year.

Czech midfielder Patrik Berger arrived from Borussia Dortmund in August 1996 and made an immediate impact with four goals in his first two games the following month.

The latest arrivals were German striker Karlheinz Riedle, also from Borussia Dortmund, who joined in time for the 1997-98 season, and American keeper Brad Friedel.

THROUGH THE YEARS
APRIL

1901
April
29

Liverpool clinched their first ever League title. Needing to win at West Bromwich Albion, who were bottom of the table, inside-right John Walker scored the first-half goal which brought the trophy to Anfield.

1914
April
25

Liverpool contested their first ever FA Cup Final. The game was played at Crystal Palace and more than 20,000 Liverpool fans made the journey. However, they were to be disappointed as Burnley ran out winners 1-0.

1980
April

Ian Rush was signed for £300,000. The man who would eventually destroy all Liverpool's scoring records had played just 33 times for Chester in the Fourth Division.

1981
April
6

Liverpool won the League Cup for the first time, beating West Ham at Villa Park after the first match had been drawn. Kenny Dalglish scored Liverpool's equaliser, and Alan Hansen the winner.

1991
April
16

Graeme Souness took over as manager. The Liverpool board had planned the appointment for the end of the season, but news leaked out, leading to Souness arriving early and taking charge for the last few games of the season which saw Liverpool finish second and qualify for a return to Europe.

1989
April
15

The month of April will always be remembered for the FA Cup Semi-Final with Nottingham Forest at Hillsborough in 1989. The much anticipated showdown ended in a scarcely believable tragedy, as a crush of Liverpool supporters at the Leppings Lane End caused 96 people to be killed. A late influx of people after the game kicked off led to massive overcrowding on the terrace, and with fences at the front preventing anybody from spilling out on to the pitch, disaster was unavoidable. In the immediate aftermath Anfield became a shrine as people came from all over the globe to lay flowers.

20 THINGS YOU PROBABLY NEVER KNEW...

1 Liverpool's first ever team did not contain a single Englishman. Similarly, when they won the Double in 1985-86, the team that clinched the FA Cup contained no English players.

2 Liverpool shared an epic FA Cup Semi-Final with Sheffield United in 1898-99. The first game finished 2-2 at Nottingham, and then 4-4 at Bolton. The third was played at Fallowfield in Manchester on a Monday afternoon. However, the ground was not able to accommodate the 30,000 spectators who kept spilling on to the pitch. The referee was forced to abandon the game after a first half which had lasted 105 minutes. Liverpool were leading 1-0, but when they tried again at Derby, the Blades scored the only goal.

3 When Liverpool met Manchester United at Old Trafford on Good Friday 1915, United won 2-0 to pick up two valuable points in their fight against relegation. However, the authorities were soon alerted to the fact that there had been a large number of bets placed around the country on that exact scoreline. An investigation eventually confirmed that the game had been fixed, and four players from each side were banned for life. The bans were lifted after the war finished, the Liverpool players being Jackie Sheldon, Bob Purcell, Tommy Miller and Tom Fairfoul.

4 The crowd at the October 1938 Merseyside derby at Goodison celebrated Prime Minister Neville Chamberlain's return from Munich and the promise of war being averted by singing the national anthem.

5 South African Berry Nieuwenhuys was suspended for life after he was found to be demanding more than £2 a game for matches during the Second World War. That was the regulation fee, but Nieuwenhuys wrote to a number of clubs setting out his what he wanted and got caught. The ban was lifted after the war and he continued to play for the club.

6 Joe Mercer, who captained Arsenal to victory over Liverpool in the 1950 FA Cup Final, was an ex-Everton player who still lived on Merseyside and regularly trained with Liverpool. When the Final approached, Mercer was still allowed at the club's training ground, but trained on his own.

7 After gracing the Football League Cup in its inaugural season of 1960-61, Liverpool did not enter it again until 1967-68 and didn't win it until 1980-81. However, they then got the taste and won it for another three consecutive years before Tottenham ended their run with a 1-0 victory in the Third Round of the 1984-85 competition.

8 Anfield was chosen as the first venue for *Match Of The Day*. The cameras recorded Liverpool beating Arsenal 3-2 on 22 August 1964, the first goal seen on the programme being scored by Roger Hunt.

9 The second leg of Liverpool's European Cup Quarter-Final against Cologne in March 1965 was abandoned as snow blanketed Anfield. When the game was eventually played, it ended goalless, as had the first leg. The teams contested a replay in Rotterdam, which finished 2-2. The game had to be decided on the toss of a coin. On the first attempt the coin stuck in the mud. On the second, Liverpool called correctly.

10 When Liverpool travelled to meet Ajax in the first leg of the First Round proper of the 1966-67 European Cup, fog reduced visibility to around 50 yards shortly before kick-off. The Italian referee was all set to call the match off, since he could not see one end of the pitch from the other, but Dutch officials managed to persuade him that the criterion in the country was being able to see the goals from the halfway line. The game was played and Ajax won 5-1, though the farce was exemplified when Bill Shankly came on to the pitch to talk to a couple of players without anybody noticing.

11 When Steve Heighway arrived at Anfield in May 1970, he was not the only graduate on the books, as team-mate Brian Hall had studied at Manchester University.

12 The first leg of the 1972-73 UEFA Cup Final against Borussia Moenchengladbach became the second European game to be postponed at Anfield. For the first encounter, Brian Hall had been picked but, in the half-hour that had been possible, Bill Shankly detected a weakness in the air in Borussia's defence and so chose John Toshack to start 24 hours later. The move was inspired as Liverpool won 3-0, picking up the trophy 3-2 on aggregate.

13 When Liverpool won the European Cup in Rome in 1977, it was a return for manager Bob Paisley who had been part of the British Army's liberating force that marched on the city at the end of the Second World War.

14 The European Cup Final of 1977 was supposed to be veteran Tommy Smith's last game for Liverpool. However, rejuvenated by the occasion and his memorable goal, he changed his mind, making another 22 League appearances before signing for Swansea City.

15 Liverpool have twice played in the World Club Championship, losing 3-0 to Brazil's Flamengo in December

1981 in Tokyo, and losing 1-0 to Independiente of Argentina in December 1984, again in Tokyo.

16 Liverpool's FA Cup Third Round replay in January 1987 with Luton had to be postponed, even though Anfield was in perfect condition. Luton were stranded in a snowstorm and couldn't reach Liverpool. The game was eventually played and finished 0-0. Liverpool lost the toss of a coin to decide the next venue, then lost 3-0 when the tie was settled at Luton's Kenilworth Road.

17 John Aldridge's failure in the 1988 FA Cup Final against Wimbledon was the first penalty miss in the fixture.

18 Graeme Souness's deficit on his transfer dealings when manager of Liverpool was £9 million.

19 Despite Souness being the manager, Ronnie Moran led the team out for the 1992 FA Cup Final. The reason was that Souness had suffered a mild heart-attack and had had an emergency bypass operation. He followed the Semi-Final in hospital and was allowed to sit on the bench for the Final, albeit with a doctor in attendance lest he get too excited.

20 Anfield has hosted a variety of football matches in which Liverpool have played no part. It was the venue for the 1977 World Cup decider between Scotland and Wales when Scotland won 2-0 to reach the Finals, as well as the 1996 play-off when Holland beat the Republic of Ireland to qualify for Euro '96. It has also hosted England internationals, Euro '96 matches and inter-league matches between the Football League and the Irish League. There have also been five FA Cup Semi-Finals. In addition, boxing was regularly staged at the ground between the wars, while professional tennis was played on boards specially laid on the pitch.

FOR CLUB AND COUNTRY

Liverpool have boasted a number of notable footballers during their history who have represented the home countries at international level, while Anfield has hosted England international matches and was a venue for Euro '96.

Liverpool's first England international was forward Harry Bradshaw, who picked up his only England cap in February 1897 against Ireland. He moved to Tottenham Hotspur a year later and died in 1899, aged just 26. Inside-left Francis Becton, who often brought the best out of Bradshaw, gained his only cap two months later.

Around the same time centre-forward George Allan became the club's first Scottish cap, gaining his only international recognition in a 2-1 victory against England. A highly talented striker, Allan scored 60 goals in 97 League and Cup matches for the Reds, helping them to the 1895-96 Division Two Championship. He left Liverpool for Celtic in 1897, returned to Liverpool within 12 months, but died a year later aged 24.

One of Liverpool's earliest star players was Scottish centre-half Alex Raisbeck. A tough defender regarded as one of the finest of his era, he won eight Scottish caps and captained Liverpool, leading them to two League Championships. He played 340 games for the Reds before becoming secretary-manager for Bristol City, Halifax and Chester. Returning to Liverpool as a scout he died in 1949.

One of Liverpool's most unusual internationals was right-half Raby Howell, who was signed from Sheffield United. He was a full-blooded gypsy, and became the first to play for England.

Right-half Maurice Parry was Liverpool's first representative for Wales, gaining 16 caps in the first decade of the century. The first Irish international was the versatile Bill Lacey, who was also the first player to move directly from Everton to Liverpool, exchanged for Tommy Gracie and Harold Uren in 1911. Lacey won international caps until he was 41, by which time he had joined New Brighton.

Liverpool's international players have always been very influential for their country. Full-back Ephraim Longworth was the first to captain his country, while Emlyn Hughes was later to skipper the national side. Three Liverpool players made the squad for England in their successful 1966 campaign. Gerry Byrne didn't play at all, Ian Callaghan played once, and Roger Hunt played in all six, scoring three times and making a significant contribution to the side's triumph.

Liverpool's most capped player is Ian Rush. The striker picked up 68 of his 73 Welsh caps while at Anfield, having made his debut against Scotland in 1980.

Emlyn Hughes is Liverpool's most capped England international, having picked up 59 caps while at Liverpool. Ray Clemence played 56 times during his stay at Anfield, adding six further appearances while with Tottenham. Phil Neal is the only other Liverpool player to have reached an England half-century, totalling exactly 50 caps.

Though born in Jamaica, John Barnes was awarded 46 England caps while on Liverpool's books. The former Watford winger made an immediate impact when he joined in 1987 along with Peter Beardsley, who was to pick up 34 caps during his time at the club. The pair arrived to help compensate for the loss of Rush to Juventus and were the creative spur behind Liverpool's title success that season.

Former captain Phil Thompson picked up 42 caps for England. He was a very slender defender and Bob Paisley joked that Thompson had tossed with a sparrow for a pair of legs and lost! He was, nevertheless, a tough tackler with considerable ability, his international caps being a testament to this. He is not the only P Thompson to have played for Liverpool as well as representing his country, outside-left Peter picking up 16 caps during the 1960s.

Two players called Kennedy have represented the Reds, and both picked up England caps. Ray Kennedy arrived from Arsenal as a striker, but found it difficult to settle. However, Bob Paisley made the inspired move of playing Kennedy in midfield, where he became an integral figure. He was capped 17 times. Alan Kennedy, no relation to Ray, picked up two England caps, making his long-awaited full debut in 1983 – nine years after first being included in the squad, when he was forced to pull out through injury! The left-back had a habit of scoring crucial international goals at club level, winning the 1981 European Cup Final with the only goal against Real Madrid and striking the decisive penalty in the shoot-out with Roma three years later.

Kenny Dalglish is the club's most-capped Scotsman, picking up 55 caps for his country while at Anfield. He played for his country on a total of 102 occasions. Considering the number of Scots to have played for Liverpool, the list of those who have earned more than ten caps is surprisingly small. Graeme Souness is second with 37, followed by Billy Liddell with 28. An Anfield stalwart who joined the club just before the Second World War, Liddell was one of the finest wingers ever to play for the club. He was also a regular goalscorer, notching 229 goals from 536 appearances. His ability was one of the reasons Liverpool's attendances were maintained when the club dropped into the Second Division in 1953-54.

One behind Liddell comes Steve Nicol, who arrived at Anfield from Ayr United in October 1981. A versatile defender, Nicol gave sterling service to Liverpool in 431 matches, and is followed on the list by fellow defender Alan Hansen with 26 caps.

After Ian Rush in the roll-call of Welsh internationals comes another tall striker, John Toshack. He represented his country 26 times during the 1970s, and also had a brief, unsuccessful spell managing the national team. Joey Jones with 18 caps is next on the list, though he won 72 in all with his other clubs: Wrexham, Chelsea and Huddersfield.

The club's most capped Irishman is midfielder Ronnie Whelan with 51, though a number of Irish players have been outstanding for Liverpool. Left-back Steve Staunton picked up 25 caps before surprisingly being sold to Aston Villa in 1991. A year later he was followed just as surprisingly by midfielder Ray Houghton, who had arrived at the club not long after Barnes and Beardsley and made a sterling contribution through his astute passing and eye for goals. Houghton was Irish in name only, having a broad Scots accent betraying his country of birth: his parentage gave him the right to wear the green of Eire

Houghton's international career will always be remembered for his heading the goal which beat England in the 1988 European Championship Finals. John Aldridge played with Houghton for both Liverpool and Ireland, though at first he found it difficult to transport his prodigious club scoring feats to the international arena.

Flying winger Steve Heighway was born of English parents in Dublin and returned to live in England when aged ten, but nevertheless opted to play international football for Ireland, earning 32 caps. A quick and athletic player with pinpoint crossing accuracy, he played 467 matches for Liverpool and was unusual among footballers in having a University degree, and today coaches the youngsters at Anfield.

Curiously, Liverpool have not had a player capped for Northern Ireland since goalkeeper Elisha Scott in 1933.

WORST SEASON 1

After achieving a glorious promotion in their first season as a Football League club, Liverpool might have expected to establish themselves in the First Division. However, their first season in the top flight was anything but easy, as the players who had served them so well in their inaugural campaign found the higher division a much harder proposition.

The 1894-95 season started with two away draws, followed by home defeats by Aston Villa and Bolton before a 5-0 drubbing was sustained at West Bromwich Albion. The ninth game of the season was the first League meeting between Liverpool and Everton and, despite all their preparations, the Reds went down 3-0 in a hard-fought encounter.

It wasn't until their next game that Liverpool were able to celebrate their first win in the First Division, with Stoke beaten 2-0 at Anfield on 20 October. However, this was not the prelude for things to come, as the next seven matches yielded four defeats and three draws, including a 2-2 draw with Everton at Anfield.

They briefly threatened a revival around Christmas and the New Year with a couple of impressive home wins (against Small Heath and West Brom), and then strung together three consecutive victories, scoring 11 goals. However, they were to win only once more all season.

With injuries and a hard winter affecting the team which had been so impressive in the previous campaign, Liverpool won just seven matches all season and lost 15, conceding 70 goals in the process. They finished bottom of a 16–team table, accumulating just 22 points.

With no automatic promotion or relegation, Liverpool took on Bury at Blackburn for the right to play in the following season's top flight. Bury's goalkeeper was sent off, but still it made little difference, as a 1-0 defeat consigned Liverpool to a return to the Second Division.

The experience probably made the club all the stronger, as their determination to bounce straight back was enormous. When they fulfilled their pledge 12 months later, the Liverpool team which graced the First Division was all the wiser for the problems it had encountered first time round and their stay in the top flight would last until 1904.

1894-95 LEAGUE RECORD

Opponents	Home	Away
Aston Villa	1-2	0-5
Blackburn Rovers	2-2	1-1
Bolton Wanderers	1-2	0-1
Burnley	0-3	3-3
Derby County	5-1	1-0
Everton	2-2	0-3
Nottingham Forest	5-0	0-3
Preston North End	2-5	2-2
Sheffield United	2-2	2-2
(Sheffield) Wednesday	4-2	0-5
Small Heath	3-1	0-3
Stoke City	2-0	1-3
Sunderland	2-3	2-3
West Bromwich Albion	4-0	0-5
Wolverhampton Wanderers	3-3	1-3

DOUBLE ACTS

Liverpool have boasted many players who have been noted for their skills when in partnership with another player as well as their individual abilities. Often putting the right players together has added something vital to the team and added an extra dimension to the ability of the players in question.

Striking partnerships have always received the most attention – and, as well as having a succession of strikers who have recorded a high number of goals for the club, the Reds have also boasted an array of notorious double acts.

Bill Shankly had tracked Motherwell striker Ian St John for some time and paid a club record £37,500 for a man who was to prove integral to Liverpool's promotion back to the First Division in 1961-62, St John's first season with the club. A gifted player in his own right, the Scot was to prove the perfect foil for record-breaking striker Roger Hunt. St John had considerable aerial ability despite his relatively small height of five feet seven and a half inches.

He scored 118 times for Liverpool in 419 appearances, an impressive enough return, but provided many more for Hunt. In their first season together, Hunt scored a record 41 League goals as Liverpool won the Second Division title. St John created a substantial proportion of those, as well as scoring 18 times himself. Hunt scored 24 League goals to St John's 19 as Liverpool re-established themselves in the top flight in 1962-63, and, when they won the Championship 12 months later, Hunt scored 31 times in the League – ten more than his strike partner. The following season saw Liverpool register their first FA Cup triumph, Hunt and St John scoring the goals which beat Leeds United.

Under Shankly, Liverpool evolved as a team and new players were integrated gradually. By 1967-68, with Hunt and St John having served a marvellous six seasons together, Shankly was beginning to look for a new pairing. He signed Tony Hateley from Chelsea, but he only stayed at Anfield for just over a year and never enjoyed the kind of understanding with Hunt that St John had.

Hunt and St John were no longer in the team in 1970-71, but Shankly finally found the two halves of Liverpool's next great striking duo. In November 1970 he paid Cardiff City £110,000 for six-foot striker John Toshack. Only 21, Toshack had been Cardiff's youngest-ever debutant and had scored 75 times for the club in 159 matches, as well as winning six Welsh caps. His partner arrived the following May for a more modest £35,000 from Scunthorpe.

The partnership took time to develop, Toshack competing for a place with Alun Evans, Brian Hall and Phil Boersma, and the following year his disappointment almost got the better of him as he signed for Leicester, only to fail the medical and return to Liverpool. However, this then sparked the pairing into life.

Toshack outscored Keegan 16 League goals to 12 in 1975-76 as Liverpool won the title and they became the most feared pairing in the country, adding a further 11 goals in other competitions. The following season Liverpool retained the League and won the European Cup, Toshack and Keegan scoring 33 goals between them.

They were never to play together again, as Keegan moved to Hamburg in June 1977 for £500,000, having scored 100 goals in his 321 matches. Toshack was not far behind, moving to Swansea City as player-manager in February 1978 where he was to mastermind the club's rise from the Fourth to the First Division.

Kevin Keegan's successor was the classy Kenny Dalglish, while Bob Paisley did not recruit a replacement in the mould of John Toshack. Instead, Ian Rush arrived in April 1980, and until Rush left for Juventus, Rush and Dalglish inherited the mantle of the partnership everybody feared. The pair notched over 300 quality goals between them, Rush's pace and clinical finishing complemented by Dalglish's astute passing and vision.

Since the heady days of Rush and Dalglish, Liverpool's striking combinations have not had the same potency. Rush and John Aldridge were too similar, though when Rush played alongside Robbie Fowler the youngster was able to learn from his experienced partner. After Stan Collymore, Michael Owen is the latest to team up with Fowler.

At the other end of the park, the partnership of Alan Hansen and Mark Lawrenson was perhaps the best and longest-standing of all. Hansen, a future Scottish international, had arrived at the club from Partick Thistle in 1977, while Lawrenson was another Liverpool transfer record, from Brighton in August 1981 for £900,000. Regarded as the finest defender in England, Lawrenson was notable for the perfect timing of his tackles.

They were an elegant and effective central pairing. During the five seasons when they played together, Liverpool collected four Championships, including the Double once, three League Cups and one European Cup. Their defensive record was excellent, and over the seasons they conceded 37 goals twice, 35 once and 32 twice.

The paring was broken up in March 1987 when Lawrenson sustained an achilles injury, only briefly to return the following season: Hansen's career came to a close in February 1991. Their partnership has recently been rekindled on TV's *Match Of The Day*.

Since Roy Evans instituted the 3–5–2 formation early in his managerial career, the attacking role of the wing-backs has become important. Jason McAteer and Stig-Inge Bjornebye have fulfilled this admirably, their forays forward proving an important creative avenue.

A midfield combination worth mentioning is John Barnes and Peter Beardsley, both of whom arrived in the summer of 1987. Barnes cost £900,000 from Watford and Beardsley a record £1.9 million from Newcastle United, but together they made Liverpool the most entertaining team in the country by a considerable margin.

Their contribution was more than just flamboyance, as Liverpool lost just two of the 40 matches they played in securing the title, playing with more flair than sides of old. They scored 87 goals in the victorious campaign, John Aldridge in particular profiting from the service. Beardsley eventually returned to Newcastle, where John Barnes replaced him in 1997 as he moved on to Bolton.

THROUGH THE YEARS
MAY

1892

May

Liverpool Football Club were formed by John Houlding. Left with an empty stadium after a split in the boardroom at Everton led to them leaving Anfield and setting up at Goodison, Houlding decided to fill the ground with a new team. Reaction at the time was one of bewilderment, as people did not see how a city could support two football teams. However Houlding, in association with John McKenna, showed how by recruiting Liverpool's first squad entirely from Scotland.

1965

May

1

May has been the month where Liverpool have collected a sizeable number of their trophies. Today, Liverpool beat Leeds United 2-1 to claim the FA Cup for the first time. Liverpool then beat Newcastle 3-0 on 4 May 1974. On 10 May 1986 Everton were beaten 3-1, allowing the Reds to claim the cup for the third time. Everton lost again on 20 May 1989, this time 3-2, and on 9 May 1992, Sunderland were beaten 2-0.

1977
May
25

All four European Cups have also been claimed in the month of May. On this date, Liverpool beat Borussia Moenchengladbach 3-1 to bring the trophy back to Merseyside. Twelve months later, Bruges were despatched 1-0 at Wembley on 10 May. On 27 May 1981 Real Madrid were beaten 1-0 in Paris, and on 30 May 1984 the club returned to Rome to defeat Roma on penalties. They also clinched their two UEFA Cups in May.

1989
May
26

However, May also has sad memories for Liverpool. In purely footballing terms, the home defeat against Arsenal robbed the Reds of the League Championship on goal difference, Arsenal claiming the title with virtually the last kick of the season.

1985
May
29

In non-football terms, off-field events before the European Cup Final between Liverpool and Juventus at the Heysel Stadium in Brussels loomed large over the club and the whole sporting world. 38 people lost their lives, and pictures were televised live across the world to a shocked public. Sanctions were swift and severe, and it would be another six seasons before Liverpool would be allowed to play in Europe again.

GREAT MIDFIELDERS

Liverpool have had a number of influential midfielders who have combined creativity with a combative nature. Many of their goals have come from such players who have proved the motor through which success was reached.

 ## TERRY McDERMOTT

L iverpool-born Terry McDermott played against the club for Newcastle United in the 1974 FA Cup Final. He was on the losing side that day, but within six months he had become new manager Bob Paisley's second signing, joining for £170,000. He took a little time to become established in the team, but finally made a significant contribution through his tireless running and his goals, often scored after well-timed late surges into the danger area.

Perhaps the most memorable of all was the final goal in the 7-0 mauling of Tottenham Hotspur at Anfield in the 1978-79 season, a perfect run and volley judged by some as the best goal ever scored at the famous venue. He also scored the crucial opening goal in Liverpool's first European Cup triumph against Borussia Moenchengladbach in 1977.

As well as four Championships, three European Cups and two League Cups, McDermott's personal worth was shown when he became the first player to win both the PFA and

Football Writers' Player of the Year awards in the same season in 1979-80. He was also capped 25 times by England.

In all, he contributed the impressive return of 75 goals in 322 appearances. He returned to Newcastle in September 1982 for £100,000 and then had brief spells in Ireland and Cyprus. His third spell at Newcastle was alongside Kevin Keegan when he took over as manager, and he remains there now under new boss Kenny Dalglish.

TERRY McDERMOTT LIVERPOOL RECORD 1974-82									
League		FA Cup		League Cup		Europe		Total	
Apps	Goals	Apps	Goals	Apps	Goals	Apps	Goals	Apps	Goals
232	54	23	4	36	5	31	12	322	75

GRAEME SOUNESS

Even though his managerial stay at Anfield was marked by controversy and a lack of success, there can be little doubt that, as a player, Graeme Souness deserves to be regarded as one of Liverpool's best midfielders. Signed from Middlesbrough for £350,000 in January 1978 he quickly became established in the side, a player of considerable skill but with a noted hard edge.

Souness helped Liverpool to five Championships, four League and three European Cups. He was influential in all three European Cup Finals in which he played, setting up Kenny Dalglish for the winning goal against Bruges in 1978, emerging on top in the battle of the hard midfielders against Real Madrid's Uli Stielike in 1981, and striking one of the penalties which won the shoot-out against Roma in 1984. He scored 56 goals from 352 appearances in all, including two European hat-tricks, but was important all over the park, as his goal-line clearance against Tottenham in the 1981-82

League Cup would testify, coming five minutes from the end of normal time with Spurs leading 1-0. Liverpool eventually claimed the trophy.

He will also be remembered for his magnanimous gesture when captain of the club in allowing manager Bob Paisley to climb the famous Wembley steps to collect the 1982-83 League Cup in Paisley's last season in charge.

Eventually he decided he needed a new challenge, signing for Italian club Sampdoria in June 1984 for £650,000. He left there for Glasgow Rangers in 1986, where he had a controversial reign as player and manager before returning to Liverpool for the end of the 1990-91 season as manager. Despite winning the FA Cup the following season, Souness' reign was not a happy one, and, with the crowd turning on him, he left the club in January 1984.

GRAEME SOUNESS LIVERPOOL RECORD 1977-84									
League		FA Cup		League Cup		Europe		Total	
Apps	Goals	Apps	Goals	Apps	Goals	Apps	Goals	Apps	Goals
247	38	24	2	45	9	36	7	352	56

 # RONNIE WHELAN

Ronnie Whelan arrived at Anfield from Dublin-based club Home Farm in October 1979. He was one of three youngsters brought over by Bob Paisley, but the only one to break into the team. His chance came in April 1981 at home to Stoke, and he took it by scoring in a 3-1 victory. He was also awarded his first international cap that month.

He and Kevin Sheedy were viewed as vying to replace Ray Kennedy in the team, and it was Whelan who eventually got the nod. Once established from the end of 1981, Whelan missed just one game and scored ten goals as the Reds took the title. He also scored the late equaliser to deny Tottenham in the 1981-82 League Cup Final, and scored again in extra-time as Tottenham eventually succumbed 3-1. The following season Liverpool retained both trophies, with Whelan grabbing a memorable Wembley winner against Manchester United.

In all Whelan helped Liverpool to six titles, three League Cups, two FA Cups and one European Cup before breaking his leg in a 3-1 defeat of Everton in February 1991, shortly before the epic Cup encounters which preceded Kenny Dalglish's resignation. As well as his vital goals, his enthusiasm and distribution were integral parts of Liverpool's success. He was appointed captain for the 1988-89 season, lifting the FA Cup but also doing an important job in congratulating the victorious Arsenal team after they had snatched the title from Liverpool's grasp at Anfield.

After recovering from injury, Whelan was in and out of the side, and was eventually released on a free transfer to Southend United, initially as a player and then also as manager. However, he was sacked as the club went down to the Second Division at the end of the 1996-97 campaign.

RONNIE WHELAN LIVERPOOL RECORD 1980-94									
League		FA Cup		League Cup		Europe		Total	
Apps	Goals	Apps	Goals	Apps	Goals	Apps	Goals	Apps	Goals
363	45	41	7	51	14	23	6	478	72

JOHN BARNES

Signed by Kenny Dalglish from Watford for £900,000, John Barnes has been one of the supreme talents to grace the post-war game in England. In his early years at the club no player could claim to generate such consistent excitement as Barnes. This marriage of excellence and reliability would make Barnes the lynchpin of a side that has frequently been in a state of flux in recent seasons.

Two Championships, an FA Cup and League Cup winner's medals came Barnes' way during his stint at the club. But while he may boast a collection of more than 70 international caps, perhaps Barnes' greatest regret will be his failure to replicate the club form that elevated him to the status of a Kop idol. He linked up with former Anfield favourite Ian Rush at Newcastle for the 1997-98 campaign and weighed in with some vital goals during the Magpies' injury crisis.

JOHN BARNES LIVERPOOL RECORD 1987-97									
League		FA Cup		League Cup		Europe		Total	
Apps	Goals	Apps	Goals	Apps	Goals	Apps	Goals	Apps	Goals
314	84	51	16	26	3	12	3	403	106

 # STEVE McMANAMAN

Steve McManaman first appeared for Liverpool as a substitute for Peter Beardsley in a December 1990 League clash with Sheffield United at Anfield. He made further substitute appearances before making his full debut against Oldham at the start of the 1991-92 campaign. McManaman played more than 50 games that season, finishing it by creating both Liverpool goals in the 2-0 FA Cup Final victory over Sunderland.

McManaman was initially played as a winger, and he has tremendous ability running at defenders. However, he now tends to play in an attacking midfield role which gives him more flexibility to pop up where he can cause most damage. It was manager Roy Evans who gave McManaman this chance at the beginning of the 1994-95 campaign with a switch to a 3-5-2 formation, and McManaman responded by becoming the creative lynchpin of Liverpool's attacks.

McManaman again starred that season at Wembley, scoring both goals as Liverpool beat Bolton 2-1 to claim the Coca-Cola Cup, and although he wasn't an influence as Liverpool lost the following season's FA Cup Final to Manchester United, his liking for Wembley was confirmed when he was a vital member of the England team which reached the semi-finals of Euro '96, earning praise from no less an authority than Pele.

McManaman is an articulate reader of the game who has written regularly for *The Times*. Sometimes criticised for his finishing, he has worked to improve this aspect of his game, and his last-minute goal against Celtic in the 1997-98 UEFA Cup, where he ran over half the length of the field before curling the ball into the corner, must rank as one of the most memorable individual goals of recent times.

STEVE McMANAMAN LIVERPOOL RECORD 1990-(97)									
League		FA Cup		League Cup		Europe		Total	
Apps	Goals	Apps	Goals	Apps	Goals	Apps	Goals	Apps	Goals
208	31	28	5	28	10	23	3	287	49

PLAYER TALK

Footballers have brains in their boots – but these Anfield favourites chose to put their thoughts into words

'It was like playing in a foreign country.'
Ian Rush on the time he spent playing with Juventus

'Bruce Grobbelaar will play on until he is 40 – and at the top level.'
Bruce Grobbelaar

'See this shirt – I'm keeping it because it will be one of my most treasured possessions. It's only just beginning to sink in that it's all over for me as a Liverpool player.'
Ian Rush after he scored at Chelsea in what should have been his last ever game for Liverpool before he left for Juventus

'There is no sentiment at Anfield. When your number is up it's up.'
Paul Walsh when he left Liverpool to join Tottenham Hotspur

'Anyone who doesn't learn from Ian Rush needs shooting.'
Robbie Fowler

'The goal looked as big as the Mersey Tunnel.'
Ian St John, reflecting on his winning goal in the 1965 FA Cup Final against Leeds United

'I don't know how I would have managed without him. It was a big step up playing in the first team, and I don't know how

I would have coped without someone keeping an eye on me and helping me out of difficult situations. I soon learned that at Liverpool, we were essentially part of a team and depended on each other.'

Ian Callaghan on backroom boy Ronnie Moran

'I said to Kevin (Keegan) "I'll go near-post" and he replied "No, just go for the ball".' *Tommy Smith*

'Sometimes I feel I'm hardly wanted in this Liverpool team. If I get two or three saves to make I've had a busy day.'

Ray Clemence

'The only thing I fear is missing an open goal in front of the Kop. I would die if that were to happen. When they start singing "You'll Never Walk Alone" my eyes start to water. There have been times when I've actually been crying while I've been playing.' *Kevin Keegan*

'I'd kick my own brother if necessary…it's what being a professional footballer is all about.' *Steve McMahon*

'After the game, I went round the chippy with my mates and got a big kiss from my mum when I got home!'

Robbie Fowler on how he celebrated scoring five goals against Fulham in 1993

'They compare Steve McManaman to Steve Heighway and he's nothing like him, but I can see why – it's because he's a bit different.' *Kevin Keegan*

'Youngsters like Michael Owen at Liverpool have shown that if you're good enough, you're old enough. The principle's not much different with me and Rushie.'

John Barnes on his 1997 transfer to Newcastle

THROUGH THE YEARS
JUNE

1977
June

Kevin Keegan broke the Kop's collective heart by joining Hamburg for £500,000. Keegan wanted the fresh challenge of a continental move, and he was a considerable success with Hamburg, twice being named European Footballer of the Year. Liverpool supporters didn't know that Keegan had told the board he wanted to play abroad at the start of the 1976-77 season, and they had said that they would agree if he was prepared to stay for one more year to help with the quest for the European Cup.

Keegan stayed and, with typical commitment, helped the club to win that trophy, as well as the League, before fulfilling his personal ambitions with the move to Germany.

1984
June
12

Fiery Scots midfielder Graeme Souness moved to Sampdoria for £650,000 having lifted the European Cup for the club the previous month. Thirteen years later to the day, Italians Torino would install Souness as manager but the appointment would be short-lived.

1995
June
17

Seeing off opposition from local rivals Everton, Liverpool set a new British transfer record when they forked out £8.5 million for Nottingham Forest striker Stan Collymore. Unfortunately, Collymore failed to settle at Anfield and was sold to Aston Villa after just two campaigns.

1987
June
9

Jamaican-born John Barnes arrived at Anfield for £900,000. It took a little time for Kenny Dalglish to secure his signature from Watford, but the form he showed in helping Liverpool to the title in his first season with the club made Barnes' acquisition a very valuable one.

1997
June
2

Oyvind Leonhardsen arrives at Anfield in a £3.5 million deal with Wimbledon. The Norwegian had impressed with his performances for the Selhurst Park outfit during 1996-97 but would take time to establish himself in the Reds' line-up following an injury.

GREAT MATCHES

Liverpool have featured in many classic matches over their history. The following five matches have been chosen as representative of many things. They mark Liverpool's success in a variety of competitions, and they celebrate the entertainment and excitement that the club has brought to English football.

Liverpool 2 Leeds United 1
1 May 1965
FA Cup Final

L iverpool's third FA Cup Final proved to be third-time lucky as the Reds triumphed to pick up the trophy for the first time. It wasn't a classic Wembley match in terms of football, but for what it meant to the club and for the bravery of one man in particular, it deserves its place among the games to remember.

Liverpool's previous two Finals had seen them lose 1-0 to Burnley at Crystal Palace in 1914 and 2-0 to Arsenal at Wembley in 1950. They had also fallen five times in the Semi-Finals. On this occasion, Chelsea were beaten 2-0 in the Semi-Final to pit them against a Leeds side who had lost out on the Championship on goal average.

The game was one of few chances and strong defending, a tense encounter as both sides vied to secure the ascendancy. However, Liverpool did create chances, and Leeds goalkeeper Gary Sprake made three excellent saves.

Liverpool had been hampered by losing Gordon Milne to injury shortly before the Final, though former Arsenal player Geoff Strong was a more than able replacement. Injury also dominated proceedings in the game, with Liverpool full-back Gerry Byrne breaking his collar-bone after five minutes of the contest. With the game being played in the era before substitutes, Byrne bravely continued as if nothing had happened. He was to be rewarded for his endeavours by creating the first goal for Roger Hunt three minutes into the first period of extra-time, the first time Liverpool had scored in a Cup Final.

Leeds were level within eight minutes through Billy Bremner, but Liverpool were not to be denied, and Ian St John's diving header in the 111th minute gave Liverpool the trophy.

The significance of the triumph was confirmed when more than half a million people lined the streets of Liverpool to welcome the victors home.

Team: Lawrence, Lawler, Byrne, Strong, Yeats, Stevenson, Callaghan, Hunt, St John, Smith, Thompson.

Wolves 1 Liverpool 3
4 May 1976
League Division One

Many Championships are won well before the end of the season, while some go right to the last game. Before television and League rulings decreed that all clubs had to play their last match simultaneously, there were a number of conclusions made all the more exciting because some clubs had finished their campaign and then had to wait to see what would prevail.

So it proved in the 1975-76 season. Liverpool had started with a 2-0 reverse at QPR and lost two of their first four away matches, but they were only to lose one further game away from Anfield for the remainder of the season. They went top after beating QPR in December, but the London side remained in contention and by the time they had finished their season, they sat on top of the table, one point ahead.

The Reds went to Molyneux ten days later requiring either a victory or a low-scoring draw to secure the title, as goal average was used to separate teams level on points. Wolves had their own problems, and needed a win to have any chance of staying in the First Division.

Nearly 50,000 were packed into Molyneux, with the gates closed an hour before kick-off, and they saw the home side take the lead in the 13th minute through Kindon. Wolves were forced to defend after that, and Liverpool went close twice through Kennedy and once through Keegan. But the Reds never gave up, and with the news coming through that Wolves' only rivals for the remaining relegation spot, Birmingham City, had equalised at Sheffield United, condemning Wolves to the drop, Liverpool finally scored the crucial goal, Keegan firing in from Toshack's header. Had the score remained 1-1, Liverpool would have claimed the title by the narrowest of margins, a goal average of 2.0645 compared to QPR's 2.0303. As it was, Toshack and Kennedy scored the goals to give them their ninth title in the most dramatic fashion by a single point.

Team: Clemence, Smith, Neal, Thompson, Kennedy, Hughes, Keegan, Case (Fairclough), Heighway, Toshack, Callaghan.

Liverpool 3 St Etienne 1
16 March 1977
European Cup Third Round second leg

In all Liverpool's long history of triumph in Europe, arguably the most unforgettable clash of all took place at Anfield during the campaign that would win the Reds their first European Cup. Drawn away to French Champions St

Etienne, Liverpool had restricted the deficit to 1-0 in a game which Kevin Keegan missed through injury. Liverpool won praise for their sensible game-plan which restricted their hosts, the beaten Finalists in the previous season's tournament, to a single goal.

Keegan returned for the match at Anfield, and he levelled the scores within two minutes, although his floated effort from the wing was probably intended more as a cross than a shot. The rest of the half saw saw Liverpool attack frantically, while St Etienne were content to play calmly on the break.

The French side levelled the match six minutes after the restart through Bathenay's 30-yard strike, meaning that Liverpool needed to score twice to progress. Ray Kennedy obliged with one but they could not grab the clinching strike despite their efforts becoming ever more frenzied. The match was also a vivid spectacle with Liverpool's red set against St Etienne's green, and the Liverpool fans matched the French fans' cries of 'Allez Les Verts' by exhorting their team with 'Allez Les Rouges'.

The stage was set for a dramatic denouement, and there has been no better man in Liverpool's history for such an occasion than David Fairclough. The man tagged 'supersub', for the number of times he had appeared from the bench to swing matches, replaced the injured John Toshack in the 72nd minute, and eight minutes from the end of the match he was set clear by Kennedy and beat two defenders before cracking the ball past the advancing keeper for the winner. Emlyn Hughes said afterwards that it was the most exciting match he had ever played in.

Team: Clemence, Neal, Jones, Smith, Kennedy, Hughes, Keegan, Case, Heighway, Toshack (Fairclough), Callaghan.

> **Liverpool 5 Nottingham Forest 0**
> **13 April 1988**
> **League Division One**

Liverpool's progression to their 17th title was imperious. Beaten just twice all season in the League, their football at times touched new heights with major arrivals John Barnes, John Aldridge, Peter Beardsley and Ray Houghton making significant contributions.

The peak of their achievements in a single game was their demolition of Nottingham Forest. Liverpool actually played Forest three times in less than a fortnight, the first being their second and last League defeat of the season, 2-1 at the City Ground, and the second a 2-1 FA Cup Semi-Final victory which took the Reds through to their shock Wembley defeat against Wimbledon.

The media reaction to the third match compared Liverpool to the Real Madrid side of the 1950s and said that Liverpool were unmatchable on that form. Former England legend Tom Finney said that it was the best performance he had ever seen. Certainly Forest could not deal with Liverpool's combination of pace, passing and imagination. Houghton gave the Reds the lead after a one-two with Barnes, and Beardsley's 30-yard pass set up Aldridge eight minutes before the interval. Defender Garry Gillespie rifled the third in the second half, Beardsley notched the fourth after Barnes' incisive run and Aldridge's second rounded things off.

Team: Grobbelaar, Ablett, Nicol, Gillespie, Hansen, Houghton (Johnston), Barnes, Spackman, McMahon (Molby), Beardsley, Aldridge.

> **Liverpool 4 Newcastle United 3**
> **3 April 1996**
> **FA Carling Premiership**

This was one of the most astonishing games ever seen at Anfield and possibly the most memorable in the short history of the Premier League. Newcastle, managed by Kevin Keegan, had led the table by a huge margin in the early part of the season and had seemed destined to win the title. However, Manchester United had eroded that lead to go top. Liverpool in third still had a chance of taking the prize, but victory over Newcastle was essential.

Robbie Fowler put the Reds in front after 97 seconds following a sweeping move, but the visitors led by half-time through goals from Les Ferdinand and David Ginola. The bare facts of the goals do scant justice to the game, as chances came and went at both ends. Robert Lee could have put the game beyond Liverpool at the start of the second half, but the Reds stormed back to equalise through Fowler.

Still both sides pressed forward and an error by David James allowed Faustino Asprilla to restore Newcastle's advantage. Back came Liverpool to equalise again, this time through record signing Stan Collymore. And just when it seemed that the game would deservedly finish all square, Barnes slipped the ball to Collymore in injury time, and he flashed a shot inside the near post to win it. The sight of Keegan and his assistant Terry McDermott almost collapsed on the bench when the goal went in will not be forgotten.

Liverpool finished in third spot, with Newcastle runners-up to Manchester United. With bookies offering odds of 1,000-1, the fixture finished in an identical scoreline the following season.

Team: James, McAteer, Jones (Rush), Scales, Wright (Harkness), Ruddock, McManaman, Redknapp, Barnes, Collymore, Fowler.

LEAGUE CUP
RECORD

It took Liverpool time to take English football's youngest Cup competition seriously – but a record four wins in a row would follow.

Stage	Opponents	Score
1960-61		
Round 2	Luton T	1-1, 5-2
Round 3	Southampton	1-2
1961-62		
Did not enter		
1962-63		
Did not enter		
1963-64		
Did not enter		
1964-65		
Did not enter		
1965-66		
Did not enter		
1966-67		
Did not enter		

Stage	Opponents	Score
1967-68		
Round 2	Bolton W	1-1, 2-3
1968-69		
Round 2	Sheffield Utd	4-0
Round 3	Swansea T	2-0
Round 4	Arsenal	1-2
1969-70		
Round 2	Watford	2-1
Round 3	Manchester C	2-3
1970-71		
Round 2	Mansfield T	0-0, 3-2
Round 3	Swindon T	0-2
1971-72		
Round 2	Hull C	3-0
Round 3	Southampton	1-0
Round 4	West Ham Utd	1-2
1972-73		
Round 2	Carlisle Utd	1-1, 5-1
Round 3	West Brom	1-1, 2-1
Round 4	Leeds Utd	2-2, 1-0
Round 5	Tottenham H	1-1, 1-3
1973-74		
Round 2	West Ham Utd	2-2, 1-0
Round 3	Sunderland	2-0
Round 4	Hull C	0-0, 3-1
Round 5	Wolves	0-1

Stage	Opponents	Score
1974-75		
Round 2	Brentford	2-1
Round 3	Bristol C	0-0, 4-0
Round 4	Middlesbrough	0-1
1975-76		
Round 2	York C	1-0
Round 3	Burnley	1-1, 0-1
1976-77		
Round 2	West Brom	1-1, 0-1
1977-78		
Round 2	Chelsea	2-0
Round 3	Derby Co	2-0
Round 4	Coventry C	2-2, 2-0
Round 5	Wrexham	3-1
Semi-Final	Arsenal	2-1, 0-0
Final	Nott'm Forest	0-0, 0-1
1978-79		
Round 2	Sheffield Utd	0-1
1979-80		
Round 2	Tranmere R	2-2, 4-0
Round 3	Chesterfield	3-1
Round 4	Exeter C	2-0
Round 5	Norwich C	3-1
Semi-Final	Nott'm Forest	0-1, 1-1
1980-81		
Round 2	Bradford C	0-1, 4-0
Round 3	Swindon T	5-0

Stage	Opponents	Score
Round 4	Portsmouth	4-1
Round 5	Birmingham C	3-1
Semi-Final	Manchester C	1-0, 1-1
Final	West Ham Utd	1-1, 2-1

1981-82

Round 2	Exeter C	5-0, 6-0
Round 3	Middlesbrough	4-1
Round 4	Arsenal	0-0, 3-0
Round 5	Barnsley	0-0, 3-1
Semi-Final	Ipswich T	2-0, 2-2
Final	Tottenham H	3-1

1982-83

Round 2	Ipswich T	2-1, 2-0
Round 3	Rotherham Utd	1-0
Round 4	Norwich C	2-0
Round 5	West Ham Utd	2-1
Semi-Final	Burnley	3-0, 0-1
Final	Manchester Utd	2-1

1983-84

Round 2	Brentford	4-1, 4-0
Round 3	Fulham	1-1, 1-1, 1-0
Round 4	Birmingham C	1-1, 3-0
Round 5	Sheffield Wed	2-2, 3-0
Semi-Final	Walsall	2-2, 2-0
Final	Everton	0-0, 1-0

1984-85

Round 2	Stockport Co	0-0, 2-0
Round 3	Tottenham H	0-1

Stage	Opponents	Score
1985-86		
Round 2	Oldham Ath	3-0, 5-2
Round 3	Brighton & HA	4-0
Round 4	Manchester Utd	2-1
Round 5	Ipswich T	3-0
Semi-Final	QPR	0-1, 2-2
1986-87		
Round 2	Fulham	10-0, 3-2
Round 3	Leicester C	4-1
Round 4	Coventry C	0-0, 3-1
Round 5	Everton	1-0
Semi-Final	Southampton	0-0, 3-0
Final	Arsenal	1-2
1987-88		
Round 2	Blackburn R	1-1, 1-0
Round 3	Everton	0-1
1988-89		
Round 2	Walsall	1-0, 3-1
Round 3	Arsenal	1-1, 0-0, 2-1
Round 4	West Ham Utd	1-4
1989-90		
Round 2	Wigan Ath	5-2, 3-0
Round 3	Arsenal	0-1
1990-91		
Round 2	Crewe Alex	5-1, 4-1
Round 3	Manchester Utd	1-3

Stage	Opponents	Score
	1991-92	
Round 2	Stoke C	2-2, 3-2
Round 3	Port Vale	2-2, 4-1
Round 4	Peterborough Utd	0-1
	1992-93	
Round 2	Chesterfield	4-4, 4-1
Round 3	Sheffield Utd	0-0, 3-0
Round 4	Crystal Palace	1-1, 1-2
	1993-94	
Round 2	Fulham	3-1, 5-0
Round 3	Ipswich T	3-2
Round 4	Wimbledon	1-1, 2-2 (3-4 pens)
	1994-95	
Round 2	Burnley	2-0, 4-1
Round 3	Stoke C	2-1
Round 4	Blackburn R	3-1
Round 5	Arsenal	1-0
Semi-Final	Crystal Palace	1-0, 1-0
Final	Bolton W	2-1
	1995-96	
Round 2	Sunderland	2-0, 1-0
Round 3	Manchester C	4-0
Round 4	Newcastle Utd	0-1
	1996-97	
Round 3	Charlton Ath	1-1, 4-1
Round 4	Arsenal	4-2
Round 5	Middlesbrough	1-2

League Cup Record Club By Club

Opposition	P	W	D	L	F-A
Arsenal	12	5	4	3	15-10
Barnsley	2	1	1	—	3-1
Birmingham C	3	2	1	—	7-2
Blackburn R	3	2	1	—	5-2
Bolton W	3	1	1	1	5-5
Bradford C	2	1	—	1	4-1
Brentford	3	3	—	—	10-2
Brighton & HA	1	1	—	—	4-0
Bristol C	2	1	1	—	4-0
Burnley	6	3	1	2	10-4
Carlisle Utd	2	1	1	—	6-2
Charlton Ath	2	1	1	—	5-2
Chelsea	1	1	—	—	2-0
Chesterfield	3	2	1	—	11-6
Coventry C	4	2	2	—	7-3
Crewe Alex	2	2	—	—	9-2
Crystal Palace	4	2	1	1	4-3
Derby Co	1	1	—	—	2-0
Everton	4	2	1	1	2-1
Exeter C	3	3	—	—	13-0
Fulham	7	5	2	—	24-5
Hull C	3	2	1	—	6-1
Ipswich T	6	5	1	—	14-5
Leeds Utd	2	1	1	—	3-2
Leicester C	1	1	—	—	4-1
Luton T	2	1	1	—	6-3
Manchester C	4	2	1	1	8-4
Manchester Utd	3	2	—	1	5-5
Mansfield T	2	1	1	—	3-2

Middlesbrough	3	1	—	2	5-4
Norwich C	2	2	—	—	5-1
Nott'm Forest	4	—	2	2	1-3
Oldham Ath	2	2	—	—	8-2
Peterborough Utd	1	—	—	1	0-1
Port Vale	2	1	1	—	6-3
Portsmouth	1	1	—	—	4-1
QPR	2	—	1	1	2-3
Rotherham Utd	1	1	—	—	1-0
Sheffield Utd	4	2	1	1	7-1
Sheffield Wed	2	1	1	—	5-2
Southampton	4	2	1	1	5-2
Stockport Co	2	1	1	—	2-0
Stoke C	3	2	1	—	7-5
Sunderland	3	3	—	—	5-0
Swansea T	1	1	—	—	2-0
Swindon T	2	1	—	1	5-2
Tottenham H	4	1	1	2	5-6
Tranmere R	2	1	1	—	6-2
Walsall	4	3	1	—	8-3
Watford	1	1	—	—	2-1
West Brom	4	1	2	1	4-4
West Ham Utd	7	3	2	2	10-11
Wigan Ath	2	2	—	—	8-2
Wimbledon	2	—	2	—	3-3
Wolves	1	—	—	1	0-1
Wrexham	1	1	—	—	3-1
York C	1	1	—	—	1-0

THE BOSS FILES

The Liverpool manager's job is the most sought after in football. We profile the men who've met that challenge over the years with ratings out of five. Anfield has seen a slow turnover in the hot seat compared with most other clubs – especially their Merseyside neighbours. The tradition in recent years has been to promote from within: every manager since Shankly has been Liverpool through and through, either as player or 'bootroom' boy.

John McKenna
1892-96

Honours: Division Two Champions   1894, 1896

McKenna was Liverpool's first boss, working in tandem with secretary-manager WE Barclay, and started a great tradition when he led them to the Second Division title with a 100 per cent home record. Immediate relegation and another Second Division title followed before McKenna stepped down but he maintained his connections with the club, serving two spells as chairman, and also worked for the FA and the League Management Committee.

Tom Watson
1896–1915

Honours: Division One Champions   1901, 1906
           Division Two Champions   1905
           FA Cup Runners-up   1914

Watson was one of the game's first big-name managers and is Liverpool's longest-serving boss. He made his reputation at Sunderland, winning three League titles, before moving to Anfield and enjoying even more success. After losing out on the Championship to Aston Villa in the final game of the 1898–99 season at Villa Park, Watson's side took the title two years later. Relegation followed in 1904 but they responded by winning the Second and First Division titles in successive seasons, the first club to achieve that feat. Apart from the 1909–10 season, Liverpool did not challenge at the top after that and Watson died in office after 19 years at the helm.

David Ashworth
1919–23

Honours: Division One Champions   1922

'Little Dave' Ashworth was Liverpool's first postwar manager and also brought silverware to Anfield. He served his apprenticeship at Oldham and Stockport and Liverpool never finished lower than fourth in the League in his reign. They won the Championship by six points in 1922 and were on course for another title triumph when he mysteriously quit to return to Oldham, who were on their way down into Division Two. He subsequently managed Manchester City and Walsall before moving into non-League football.

Matt McQueen
1923–28

Honours: Division One Champions   1923

McQueen was the first former Liverpool player to take charge of the side when he replaced Ashworth and confirmed the Reds as the 1923 League Champions. A former Scottish international right-half and Football League linesman who had spells as Liverpool goalkeeper and a club director, McQueen could not live up to the illustrious reputation of his predecessors though he always kept the side comfortably in mid-table. He was forced into retirement by illness.

George Patterson
1928–36

Honours: None

Patterson set the tone for future Liverpool managers by taking charge after 20 years as assistant manager. The side he inherited from Ashworth continued to jog along in mid-table, flirting twice with relegation, but he groomed some useful youngsters including Matt Busby. He earned a League long-service award after 21 years at Anfield.

George Kay
1936–51

Honours: Division One Champions   1947
            FA Cup Runners-up   1950

Kay had the difficult task of resurrecting Liverpool after World War II and did it in style as he led them to the first postwar Championship. After a career with Bolton, West

Ham and Stockport, he worked at Luton and managed Southampton before arriving on Merseyside. His title-winning season was followed by indifferent League form, but some sparkling Cup runs from his attacking side saw an appearance in the Final and another in the Semis. He finally had to quit on medical grounds.

Don Welsh
1951–56

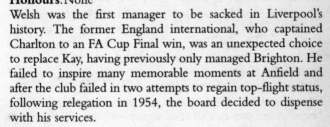

Honours: None

Welsh was the first manager to be sacked in Liverpool's history. The former England international, who captained Charlton to an FA Cup Final win, was an unexpected choice to replace Kay, having previously only managed Brighton. He failed to inspire many memorable moments at Anfield and after the club failed in two attempts to regain top-flight status, following relegation in 1954, the board decided to dispense with his services.

Phil Taylor
1956–59

Honours: None

Taylor was a former Liverpool captain and ex-England international who did everything but take them back into the top flight in his time in charge. His three full seasons saw them finish third, fourth and fourth in Division Two and they were heading for another third-place finish when he resigned due to ill health. The low point of his tenure was an FA Cup defeat at non-League Worcester in 1959.

LIVERPOOL

Bill Shankly
1959-74

Honours: Division One Champions   1964, 1966, 1973
Division Two Champions   1962
FA Cup Winners   1965, 1974
UEFA Cup Winners   1973
Cup Winners' Cup Runners-up 1966

The legendary Shankly is arguably the most famous manager there has ever been in football. He turned Liverpool into one of the most successful club sides in the world in his 16-and-a-half year stint in charge and even now is spoken of in reverential tones by his former players and Liverpool fans.

When he arrived at the club they were still trying to escape the Second Division, but within five years of his appointment he had won them the League title and reached an FA Cup Semi-Final. Liverpool went on to dominate English and European football in the 1960s and 1970s and even after he retired his legacy lived on as the trophies continued to arrive at Anfield. Shankly was a Scottish international as a player and managed Carlisle, Grimsby, Workington and Huddersfield before joining Liverpool.

He won the OBE for his services to the game and his death plunged the whole football world into mourning, so much so that almost every English League club was represented at his funeral.

Bob Paisley
1974–83

Honours:	Division One Champions	1976, 1977, 1979, 1980, 1982, 1983
	FA Cup Runners-up	1977
	League Cup Winners	1981, 1982, 1983
	European Cup winners	1977, 1978, 1981
	UEFA Cup Winners	1976

One of the most successful managers of all time, Paisley handled the almost impossible job of following Shankly in his own quiet way. After 17 years on the backroom staff, Paisley, a former Liverpool player, led them to 13 trophies in just nine years in charge and signed players like Kenny Dalglish and Graeme Souness. After retiring he stayed on in an advisory role and also had a spell on the board.

Joe Fagan
1983–85

Honours:	Division One Champions	1984
	League Cup Winners	1984
	European Cup Winners	1984
	European Cup Runners-up	1985

Fagan was another who made the transition from the bootroom to the manager's chair, replacing Paisley after nine years as his assistant. He led Liverpool to the Treble of the European Cup, League Championship and League Cup in his first season. Tragically his last game in charge was the European Cup Final against Juventus in the Heysel Stadium where 38 people died. Fagan played for Manchester City and Bradford PA and was player-manager of Nelson before becoming Rochdale's trainer, a role he also undertook at Anfield.

Kenny Dalglish
1985-91

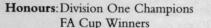

Honours: Division One Champions   1986, 1988, 1990
FA Cup Winners   1986, 1989
League Cup Runners-up   1987

Kop favourite Kenny Dalglish was Liverpool's first player-manager and became the first ever to win the League and FA Cup Double at the end of his first season in charge. He played his part on and off the pitch, scoring the goal that decided the Championship at Chelsea. The FA Cup Final defeat by Wimbledon in 1988 cost him another Double and it was the other way round a year later when Arsenal deprived them of the title after they had beaten Everton in the Cup Final. He surprisingly resigned in February 1991 due to stress, two days after a 4-4 FA Cup draw at Everton, but re-emerged eight months later at Blackburn, who he led to the Premiership title. The former Scotland and Celtic striker is currently manager of Newcastle.

Graeme Souness
1991-94

Honours: FA Cup Winners   1992

Souness returned to Anfield, where he had been such a force as a player, from the manager's job at Rangers. He had a turbulent time as boss, with just an FA Cup Final win and two trips into Europe to keep the fans happy, and needed heart surgery in April 1992. The former Scotland international survived enormous pressure from inside and outside the club before eventually resigning.

Roy Evans
1994–

Honours: League Cup Winners   1995
              FA Cup Runners-up   1996

Evans was another who worked his way through the
Liverpool ranks to end up in the manager's hotseat. In the
1996-97 season he was criticised by fans for the club's
apparent lack of success but he resolutely declared he would
see the job through. Although the Reds have not won the
League since 1990, Evans has brought silverware to Anfield
with a League Cup win in 1995, and he also took them to
within a whisker of the 1997 Cup Winners' Cup Final.

BEST SEASON 2

Liverpool finally captured the Double of League Championship and FA Cup in 1985–86, Kenny Dalglish's first campaign in charge.

The season was played in the shadow of the Heysel disaster, and Liverpool were banned from Europe. Neighbours Everton, their rivals for both major trophies that season, were also suffering from the ban, having lost their chance of contesting the European Cup.

Changes to the Liverpool squad included the departures of full-backs Phil Neal and Alan Kennedy, while former midfielder Steve McMahon arrived from Villa. Dalglish himself was not in the team to start off with, preferring to partner Ian Rush with Paul Walsh.

Liverpool's opening to the season was not spectacular, and by Christmas they were fourth. Manchester United had opened the campaign with ten straight wins, but they ran out of steam and it was Everton who took over at the top.

The Championship appeared lost in February when Everton won 2-0 at Anfield and looked the best side in the country. Their lead was six points and they had a game in hand. Yet Liverpool didn't give up and put an unbeaten run together while Everton began to falter. Eventually the title came down to the last game of the season, Liverpool knowing that a win at Stamford Bridge would secure the Championship. It was not going to be easy, though, especially as Chelsea had already secured a draw at Anfield earlier in the campaign. However, with Dalglish now back in the side, Liverpool weren't going to miss out, and it was the manager who sealed the title with a neat volley.

In the FA Cup, Liverpool opened their run with a 5-0 win at home to Norwich before winning a tricky tie 2-1 at Chelsea. They met York City in the Fifth Round for the second season running, winning 3-0 in a replay, before travelling to Watford. Their run may well have ended here, with the first match ending 0-0 at Anfield and Liverpool heading out of the competition in the replay, trailing 1-0 right at the death. However, Jan Molby converted a late penalty, and Ian Rush secured victory in extra-time. Rush was then on target twice to beat Southampton in the Semi-Final.

So to Wembley and the long-cherished dream of an all-Merseyside Final. Liverpool emerged 3-1 winners, having trailed at half-time, to deny their neighbours another trophy and claim their first Double.

1985-86 LEAGUE RECORD

Opponents	Home	Away
Arsenal	2-0	0-2
Aston Villa	3-0	2-2
Birmingham City	5-0	2-0
Chelsea	1-1	1-0
Coventry City	5-0	3-0
Everton	0-2	3-2
Ipswich Town	5-0	1-2
Leicester City	1-0	2-0
Luton Town	3-2	1-0
Manchester City	2-0	0-1
Manchester United	1-1	1-1
Newcastle United	1-1	0-1
Nottingham Forest	2-0	1-1
Oxford United	6-0	2-2
Queens Park Rangers	4-1	1-2
Sheffield Wednesday	2-2	0-0
Southampton	1-0	2-1
Tottenham Hotspur	4-1	2-1
Watford	3-1	3-2
West Bromwich Albion	4-1	2-1
West Ham United	3-1	2-2

THE GROUND

Liverpool's home at Anfield will always hold a place in football history for coining the phrase 'Kop'. The huge covered terrace, built for the start of the 1906–07 season was called the 'Spion Kop' by a local sports journalist, and although Arsenal fans had used the same name for a terrace at one of their previous grounds it was this that spawned the common use of the phrase.

Anfield was originally built for Everton, and Liverpool were only formed after a boardroom split in 1892. Everton moved out and left John Houlding to establish a new club based at the ground.

There must have been far worse places for a fledgling club to start life. The ground held around 20,000 people at the time, and had staged an England international three years earlier. The Anfield Road End had uncovered accommodation for 4,000 fans while the rest of the ground boasted two smaller stands and a pavilion, which were fairly common at stadia around that time.

The ground saw few changes over the next decade until major building works in 1906 changed the face of Anfield for ever. The Kop was built at the south end of the ground while the traditional Main Stand, with an enclosure in front of it, was also constructed. Covers had already been placed over the other two sides three years earlier and a roof was placed on the Kop in 1928. Improvements to the famous terrace boosted its capacity to 30,000.

Little else happened to Anfield for over 35 years until in 1963 the Kemlyn Road Stand, opposite the Main Stand, was rebuilt. Two years later the club replaced the crumbling Anfield Road End with a new terrace and roof and in 1970 increased the number of seats in the Main Stand.

By the middle of the 1980s the capacity had dropped from over 50,000 in the 1970s to around 45,000 after the enclosure and the Anfield Road End were seated, leaving the Kop and a corner section between Anfield Road and Kemlyn Road as the only terracing in the ground.

The Kemlyn Road Stand was completely demolished and rebuilt in the early 1990s, a lot later than the club hoped after problems persuading some of the residents who lived in the street to move to new homes, and was renamed the Centenary Stand – but the biggest change occurred in 1994 when fans were able to stand on the Kop for the last time. The Heysel and Hillsborough tragedies and the resultant Taylor report had numbered the days for terracing and, despite protests from some fans, the Kop's time was up. Norwich were the visitors on an emotional afternoon and they spoilt the party by winning 1-0.

The new Kop holds 12,000 fans and sits opposite a new structure at the Anfield Road End which was built in 1997. The old stand was knocked down in the summer and the work rumbled on into the new season, meaning the club had to exclude away fans from the first few games of the campaign. The first visiting supporters to use some of the new facilities were from Celtic in a UEFA Cup tie towards the end of October. This work limited Anfield's capacity to 35,000 at the beginning of the season but that was due to rise to 45,000 if the work was completed on time in February 1998.

Although the ground missed out on staging matches in the 1966 World Cup Finals it proved a suitable venue for Euro '96, hosting four games including the Quarter-Final where France beat Holland 5-4 on penalties.

THROUGH THE YEARS
JULY

1974
July
12

When a Liverpool press conference was called, it appeared to be solely about the record signing of Ray Kennedy from Arsenal for £200,000. However, the real news of the day was that Bill Shankly had announced his retirement from management. Shankly had decided to retire while still at the top, even though he had been offered whatever salary he chose to remain.

As well as winning Liverpool's promotion back to the First Division, 'Shanks' had also won three League Championships, the FA Cup and the UEFA Cup, while revolutionising the way Liverpool were run and laying the foundations of the club that would dominate English football for two decades. The succession was handled smoothly, Bob Paisley being elevated to the position of manager while others behind the scenes also rose one rung up the boot-room 'ladder'.

1983
July
4

Following Bob Paisley's retirement, new boss Joe Fagan allows 'supersub' David Fairclough to leave Anfield for Lucerne of

Switzerland. Unusually Fagan hadn't played for Liverpool, despite being born in the city. Instead he played nearly 150 games for Manchester City before a broken leg curtailed his career, even though he continued playing with Bradford Park Avenue and various non-League sides. He joined Liverpool as an assistant trainer in 1958 and was 62 when he took the top job. His first campaign in charge saw Liverpool claim a hat-trick of trophies, but they won none the following season when Fagan retired in great sadness following the events of Heysel.

1987
July
13

Nippy Newcastle striker Peter Beardsley arrived for a record £1.9 million. He formed a highly effective understanding with another new arrival, ex-Watford midfielder John Barnes.

1993
July
21

Having overcome the obstacle of Spurs refusing to pay Neil Ruddock a loyalty bonus for his one season at White Hart Lane, Liverpool agree a £2.5 million transfer fee. The rugged defender would become a cult hero at Anfield but would be forced to endure several spells on the sidelines due to the fierce competition for places.

ATTENDANCES

Liverpool have always been one of the best-supported clubs in England with their average attendance almost always above the average for their division.

Their first-ever League season saw around 5,215 spectators pass through the Anfield turnstiles for every home game in Division Two, the second highest crowd in the division behind Woolwich Arsenal. The crowds had grown to over 12,000 the following season, their first in Division One, but dropped once more to 5,795 with relegation.

Another instant promotion saw gates return to more than 12,000 a game and by the turn of the century over 15,000 people were flocking to Anfield every other week. A record average home crowd of 21,620 was established in 1909–10 as Liverpool finished runners-up in the League, and by the end of the First World War their average had shot up to nearly 30,000.

In 1922–23 Liverpool could proudly boast they were the best side in the land and the best-supported one as well with England's highest average attendance of 33,495 cheering them to their second consecutive League Championship.

Crowds hovered between the 20,000 and 30,000 mark from then until World War II but after the end of hostilities, crowds streamed to football in ever-increasing numbers. The first full peacetime season in 1946–47 saw 45,732 watching George Kay's Championship-winning side in action at Anfield home games, with only Newcastle commanding more pulling power.

The average crowd rarely dropped below 36,000 in the following seasons despite the lack of further silverware, and in the 1960s Merseyside had two of the most popular sides in the country, with both Liverpool and Everton two of the top three sides with the highest average home attendances for nine consecutive seasons.

Liverpool topped the tree yet again in 1965-66, coincidentally another Championship campaign, with average home crowds of 46,344 and also led the way in 1970-71, 1971-72, 1987-88 and 1988-89, although they won the title in only one of those campaigns. For the rest of the 1970s, 1980s and 1990s, with the exception of three seasons, Liverpool's crowds were second only to those of arch-rivals Manchester United, though both clubs had to cut their capacities due to ground redevelopment.

Liverpool's record attendance figure is unlikely to ever be broken unless the club plan some major ground rebuilding or leave Anfield. On 2 February 1952, 61,905 people squeezed into the ground to see an FA Cup Fourth Round tie with Wolves. Most of them went home happy as Liverpool won 2-1, but their joy was short-lived as Burnley beat them 2-0 in the next round.

The club's record receipts, not surprisingly, came from a more recent game as a crowd of paid £496,000 to see a Fourth Round Coca-Cola Cup tie with Newcastle on 29 November 1995 which the Reds lost 1-0. That figure is sure to be broken with the ever-increasing price of admission.

The lowest crowd thought to have watched League football at Anfield is the 1,000 who saw the 1-0 Second Division win over Loughborough on 7 December 1895.

European nights have always generated a superb atmosphere around Anfield and a huge crowd inside the ground. It is up to Roy Evans to ensure such glory games continue to generate the revenue on which Liverpool depend to fund future development.

DREAM TEAM 2

In 1984, Liverpool were to complete their first ever hat-trick of title successes, as well as lifting the League Cup and the European Cup. Most of the players won Championships and League Cups in the early 1980s and formed the majority of the side which won the Double in 1986.

GROBBELAAR
1

NEAL
2

HANSEN
6

LAWRENSON
4

KENNEDY
3

LEE
8

WHELAN
5

SOUNESS
11

JOHNSTON
10

DALGLISH
7

RUSH
9

Goalkeeper   **Bruce Grobbelaar**
Grobbelaar was the eccentric Zimbabwe goalkeeper who
played over 600 matches for Liverpool and entertained as
much as he protected. The penalty shoot-out against Roma
was one of his finest performances, as his moments of
clowning unnerved Roma's players so much they missed the
target.

Right-back   **Phil Neal**
Neal was Bob Paisley's first signing and rarely missed a match
until he left the club towards the end of 1985. His cool
penalty-taking complemented his effective defensive work.

Central defender   **Alan Hansen**
Hansen was the man who would shortly captain Liverpool to
further glory. At his peak he was one of the best defenders in
the game, and the Scots international returned from serious
injury to play again towards the end of the 1980s

Central defender   **Mark Lawrenson**
Lawrenson was an elegant central defender regarded by many
as the best of his day. His career was cruelly cut short by
injury, but he formed an impressive and successful rearguard
with Alan Hansen for five years.

Midfielder   Ronnie Whelan

Whelan contributed to Liverpool for more than a decade, scoring vital goals and working both in defence and attack.

Left-back   Alan Kennedy

Kennedy was a solid defender who had a habit of scoring vital goals, not least the decisive penalty in the Roma shoot-out. He had also won the 1981 European Cup with a clever finish after a run forward. He and Neal left Liverpool within three months of one another.

Striker   Kenny Dalglish

Dalglish's list of achievements as player and manager following his 1977 arrival from Scottish Champions Celtic is enormous, and he is one of the club's all-time greats. He was substituted in the Roma match.

Midfielder   Sammy Lee

Liverpudlian Lee was a great enthusiast who made a large contribution in the early 1980s, sharing in all the club's successes. However, he lost form in 1984-85 and was eventually transferred to QPR.

Striker   **Ian Rush**

Record-goalscorer Rush enjoyed a particularly prolific 1983-84, scoring 47 times in all, including two goals in Romania to beat Dinamo Bucharest in the European Cup Semi-Final.

Midfielder   **Craig Johnston**

Australian Johnston was born in South Africa, and his passing and eye for goal kept him in the Liverpool team during the 1980s. However he became disillusioned with the game and announced his retirement in 1988 at the early age of 27.

Midfielder   **Graeme Souness**

Souness's last act as a Liverpool player was to lift the 1984 European Cup. The dominating midfielder who had contributed so much in his six years signed for Sampdoria in the summer.

LFC Trivia Quiz

**Test your Anfield knowledge.
Answers on page 190-191.**

1   Which goalkeeper understudied Ray Clemence for four years, making just four appearances, before establishing himself as a top-flight goalkeeper with Coventry City?

2   The father of which Liverpool striker of the 1990s played for the club in the 1950s?

3   Which striker scored on his Liverpool debut at Old Trafford in 1991 but was sold after starting just nine League matches?

4   Against which club did Stan Collymore make a goalscoring debut?

5   From which club did Graeme Souness sign Rob Jones?

6   Which team knocked Liverpool out of the 1978-79 European Cup, ending a run which had seen them win the trophy twice?

7   Why was Jan Molby not available for selection towards the end of 1988?

8   How many times have Liverpool won the Charity Shield, including occasions when they have shared it?

9   Which striker scored three consecutive League hat-tricks for the club?

10   Who scored the Reds' winning goal against Blackburn in the last game of the 1994–95 season when Rovers clinched the title at Anfield following Manchester United's failure to win at West Ham?

11   Against which team did Liverpool score ten goals in a week in the 1995-96 season?

12   Which was the first European team to win at Anfield?

13   Which Scottish midfielder was Liverpool's leading scorer in the 1984-85 season?

14   Which players went to West Ham as part of the deal which brought Julian Dicks to Anfield?

15   Which former Liverpool star was sacked as reserve team coach in 1992?

16   Against which club did Liverpool win a penalty shoot-out to reach the 1992 FA Cup Final?

17   Who was Joe Fagan's first signing as manager of Liverpool.

18   Which two players scored hat-tricks in Liverpool's 10-1 victory against Oulun Palloseura in the First Round of the 1980-81 European Cup?

19   Which two defenders were signed in the 1994-95 season for a combined cost of £7 million?

20   Which player had a goal disallowed in the 1988 FA Cup Final because the referee had blown for an earlier infringement?

21   Why did Bruce Grobbelaar make no attempt to save Alan Smith's goal for Arsenal at Anfield on the night the Gunners clinched the title through Michael Thomas?

22   Against which club did Liverpool play a friendly for their first match after the Hillsborough tragedy?

23   Which former Liverpool player managed Brighton to a shock victory over Liverpool in the 1982–83 FA Cup?

24   Who were the only three teams to beat Liverpool across all competitions in the 1987–88 Championship season?

25   How many League matches did winger Jimmy Carter play for Liverpool, including substitute appearances?

26   What was the score when Ian Rush returned to Anfield with Leeds United in the 1996–97 season?

27   Who was Liverpool's leading scorer for five consecutive seasons in the 1930s?

28   Which former Glasgow Rangers winger made his Liverpool debut as a substitute against Oldham in 1991?

29   Against which country did Steve McManaman make his international debut?

30 Against which club did Robbie Fowler score his first League hat-trick?

31 How many goals did Ian Rush score for Liverpool in FA Cup Finals?

32 What is the name of Liverpool's training ground?

33 Against which club did Ronnie Whelan score his only Liverpool hat-trick?

34 Which team did Liverpool beat to win the European Super Cup in 1977-78?

35 How many FA Cup Semi-Finals have been played at Anfield?

36 Which Liverpool band had a Number 1 hit with 'You'll Never Walk Alone' which led to the song being adopted by the Kop?

37 Which two future Liverpool players were part of Oxford's victorious League Cup team in 1986?

38 What was the attendance at Liverpool's first ever League match?

39 Who is the only player other than Ian Rush to have scored for Liverpool in more than one FA Cup Final?

40 Which two Liverpool players have left the club to become player-manager of Swansea?

THROUGH THE YEARS
AUGUST

1946
August
31

Legendary winger Billy Liddell joined Liverpool before the Second World War, but despite guesting for them during the conflict, he didn't make his official League debut until today at Sheffield United.

1964
August
22

The cameras of *Match Of The Day* made their first visit anywhere in 1964, appearing at Anfield to record Liverpool's 3-2 victory over Arsenal. The new, cantilevered Kemlyn Road stand was opened on the same day. The stand had a capacity of 6,700.

1977
August

Kenny Dalglish arrived at Anfield for a record £440,000 to replace Kevin Keegan. He would prove to be Bob Paisley's greatest ever signing, topping 100 goals for Liverpool, forming a deadly partnership with Ian Rush which led to a string of trophies in the 1980s.

1974
August
10

Liverpool have appeared in a record 17 Charity Shields during August. Memorable games include the 1974 tussle with Leeds United, the first time Liverpool had contested the shield at Wembley, and Kevin Keegan and Billy Bremner were sent off. Unusually the shield was not shared, Liverpool winning 6-5 on penalties after a 1-1 draw.

1988
August
20

Champions Liverpool took revenge on Wimbledon for the Cup Final defeat that cost them the Double by beating the Londoners 2-1.

1992
August
8

Liverpool's most recent appearance in the Charity Shield was against Leeds United, when an Eric Cantona hat-trick consigned them to a 4-3 defeat.

TRANSFERS

The ever-spiralling cost of professional footballers has seen Liverpool smash their transfer record four times in the 1990s.

Dean Saunders started the trend in July 1991 when he moved from Derby for £2.9 million. However, despite finishing as Liverpool's leading scorer in his first season with ten League strikes and some crucial Cup goals, including four against Kuuysi Lahti and a hat-trick against Swarovski Tirol in the UEFA Cup, he was sold to Aston Villa just 15 months later at a £600,000 loss.

Two years later, Liverpool were breaking the bank again as they paid a British record fee for a defender of £3.6 million to sign Republic of Ireland international Phil Babb from Coventry. Babb had just played a key role in his country's run to the second stage of the 1994 World Cup Finals, appearing in every one of their five games in the United States.

He had earned rave reviews for his performances and seemed an inspired signing. Although not always popular with some sections of the Anfield crowd, Babb has performed a sterling job despite losing his regular place to Bjorn Tore Kvarme and having to settle for a place on the bench.

Less than a year after Babb's arrival his fee was dwarfed by the £8.5 million signing of striker Stan Collymore from Nottingham Forest. The British record fee proved a bit much for Collymore to handle at times and he had an inconsistent two years at Anfield. He never really established a regular starting place in the side although when he did play he both scored goals and set them up for his striking partner Robbie

Fowler. He eventually moved to Aston Villa for £7 million in the summer of 1997, becoming another record signing who Liverpool failed to sell on for a higher fee.

Turning the clock back to another era, Liverpool got a much better deal out of some of their earlier record buys. Kenny Dalglish joined the club from Celtic in 1977 for what was then a British record fee of £440,000 and hit 30 League and Cup goals in his first season. He went on to become player-manager in 1985 and stayed with the club until 1991 when he resigned. He scored more than 160 goals in nearly 500 games for the club and certainly proved value for money.

So did John Toshack, who was Liverpool's most expensive purchase when he moved from Cardiff in November 1970 for £110,000. The Welsh international striker formed a deadly partnership with Kevin Keegan during his eight-year stay at Anfield and helped the club to a string of trophies, including three League titles, scoring 95 goals.

Toshack's fee was eclipsed by the £180,000 Bill Shankly paid Arsenal for striker Ray Kennedy, his last act before retiring. His successor Bob Paisley converted Kennedy to a midfielder and it proved a shrewd move as the player made more than 300 appearances as the club collected trophies.

The advent of the Bosman ruling has made it possible for clubs to get European players on the cheap. Liverpool have used the rule to their advantage to sign Bjorn Tore Kvarme and Jorgen Nielsen but found problems when trying to bring in American goalkeeper Brad Friedel.

Arguably the biggest bargain buy in Liverpool's history was Kevin Keegan who cost just £35,000 from Scunthorpe in 1971 and went on to help the club win every honour in the book and be named Footballer of the Year in his time at Anfield. He later joined Hamburg for £500,000 – a good piece of business by any yardstick.

WORST SEASON 2

Despite winning the League title in 1946–47, Liverpool were to begin a decline which culminated in relegation in 1953–54. It was a surprise that the dip should be so sudden, but many of the Liverpool players who won the title had then been at their peak – and as their performance dropped so, inevitably, did that of the team.

Having narrowly avoided relegation in the previous campaign, the portents were not good for the Reds in August 1953 – and so the season proved. Liverpool recorded just nine victories from 42 matches and conceded 97 goals, scoring 68. They finished bottom of the First Division with 28 points, and their disappointment was increased as Everton were runners-up in the Second Division in the same season and passed them going down.

The Reds won seven times at Anfield, and the manner of the victories was impressive, including a 6–1 triumph against Aston Villa, a 5–2 defeat of Blackpool and a 4–0 victory over Burnley. They drew eight matches, including a 4–4 draw with Manchester United, and lost the remainder. It was really on their travels that Liverpool came unstuck, winning just twice – 2–0 at Manchester City and 1–0 at Middlesbrough, though these wins came within ten days of one another. There were some very heavy defeats in the 17 they suffered away from home, including a 6–0 reverse at Charlton, a 5–1 defeat at Manchester United and two 5–2 defeats at Chelsea and West Brom.

Relegation was confirmed on 10 April when Liverpool went down 3-0 at Arsenal – a match which saw opposing captain Joe Mercer break his leg, never to return to action.

Liverpool used 31 players during the campaign and, apart from Billy Liddell with 36 appearances, the next highest total was Laurie Hughes with 27: this showed that team selection was inconsistent throughout the season. Sammy Smyth and Louis Bimpson were top scorers with 13 goals each, but from just 26 and 24 matches respectively. Bob Paisley played 20 matches but retired from playing at the end of the season.

It had to get worse before it could get better for Liverpool, and they finished the next season 11th in the Second Division – their lowest ever League placing. In all, they languished in the lower division for eight seasons.

1953-54 LEAGUE RECORD

Opponents	Home	Away
Arsenal	1-2	0-3
Aston Villa	6-1	1-2
Blackpool	5-2	0-3
Bolton Wanderers	1-2	0-2
Burnley	4-0	1-1
Cardiff City	0-1	1-3
Charlton Athletic	2-3	0-6
Chelsea	1-1	2-5
Huddersfield Town	1-3	0-2
Manchester City	2-2	2-0
Manchester United	4-4	1-5
Middlesbrough	4-1	1-0
Newcastle United	2-2	0-4
Portsmouth	3-1	1-5
Preston North End	1-5	1-2
Sheffield United	3-0	1-3
Sheffield Wednesday	2-2	1-1
Sunderland	4-3	2-3
Tottenham Hotspur	2-2	1-2
West Bromwich Albion	0-0	2-5
Wolverhampton Wanderers	1-1	1-2

A-Z OF LIVERPOOL

**The Anfield story, alphabetically speaking, is
one of S for success, from goal ace John
Aldridge to Bruce Grobbelaar's adopted
country Zimbabwe!**

A John Aldridge's last goal for Liverpool was a penalty in the
9-0 drubbing of Crystal Palace in September 1989. It was his
first touch of the match having just come on as a substitute.
At the end of the game, the tearful Scouse striker threw his
shirt into the Kop, and the following day signed for Real
Sociedad. Bought as a replacement for Ian Rush, Aldridge
scored 61 times in just 102 matches. He fulfilled his dream of
playing for his home-town club and scored some memorable
goals, particularly in the 1989 FA Cup victory over Everton.

B Phil Boersma played just under 100 games for Liverpool in
the 1960s and 1970s, but became a controversial figure when
Graeme Souness appointed him as his assistant on taking over
as manager at Anfield. Previous managers had worked with
the existing backroom staff, and the appointment caused
confusion. He was replaced by Roy Evans at the end of the
1992-93 season as the Liverpool board's condition on Souness
remaining as manager.

C Full-back Tom Cooper, an England international, was
killed in June 1940 when his motorbike collided with a bus.

D Left-half Joe Dines only made one appearance for
Liverpool but played 27 amateur internationals, winning an
Olympic gold medal in 1912.

E Alun Evans was a striker of considerable potential who arrived at Anfield from Wolves in September 1968, the £100,000 fee a record for a teenager. His ability was highlighted by a hat-trick against Bayern Munich in the 1970-71 Fairs Cup. However, he was attacked in a Midlands nightclub and required facial surgery to repair his injuries. He lost his confidence, became prone to injury and was eventually transferred to Aston Villa in June 1972, having scored 33 times in 110 appearances.

F Joe Fagan was at Anfield for 26 years before being appointed manager.

G Liverpool-born Howard Gayle started just three League matches in his six years at the club, appearing once more as a substitute. His only other appearance was as a substitute in the European Cup Semi-Final second leg away to Bayern Munich. Bayern knew nothing about him, and his running at the defence swung the game Liverpool's way. His efforts did not, however, earn him any more European matches.

H Andrew Hannah and David Hannah both played for Liverpool in the 1890s but were not related, while in the following decade the unrelated Jim Hughes and John Hughes played at the same time in a move to confuse the club's fans.

I Forward Alan Irvine cost £75,000 from Falkirk in 1986 but managed just four substitute appearances for Liverpool before leaving for Dundee United.

J Reverend James Jackson played over 200 games for Liverpool in the 1920s and 1930s, the money helping to fund his studies to become a minister. He was finally ordained in 1933 and was nicknamed 'Parson' by the Liverpool fans.

K Kevin Keegan was the first Englishman to be sent off at Wembley, dismissed for fighting with Billy Bremner in the 1974 Charity Shield.

L Goalkeeper Tommy Lawrence, a fine Liverpool custodian during the successful 1960s, was known as 'Flying Pig' by the Kop due to his size. For a time his understudy was John Ogston, who had been known as 'Tubby' while at Aberdeen.

M Ronnie Moran joined Liverpool in January 1952 after being recommended by a postman who had one of the club's directors on his round. Moran has proved to be a valuable and loyal contributor to Liverpool, playing 379 matches before joining the coaching staff. He briefly took over as manager when Dalglish resigned, holding the fort for Souness.

N Centre-half Robert Neil, who played for Liverpool in the 1890s, was just five foot four inches tall.

O Michael Owen scored on his League debut at Wimbledon in April 1997 after coming on as substitute, making him the youngest to score for Liverpool at 17 years and five months.

P Two Fred Perrys have played at Anfield. The three-times Wimbledon Champion played tennis at the ground between the wars, while a right-back made his only appearance in a 2-1 defeat against Blackburn on 31 December 1955.

Q Queen Mary was one of the first royal visitors to Anfield, accompanying King George V to the 1921 FA Cup Semi-Final between Wolverhampton Wanderers and Cardiff.

R At the end of 1953, Liverpool boasted an Anthony and an Antonio Rowley on their books. The former was an inside-left known by his second name of Arthur, while the second was born in Wales of Italian extraction and was known as Tony. He was an inside-right who scored a hat-trick on his debut in a 3–2 victory over Doncaster in August 1954.

S Goalkeeper Cyril Sidlow, who played for the club immediately after the Second World War, was noted for his excellent distribution skills and was one of the first goalkeepers to throw the ball to his colleagues rather than simply kicking it downfield.

T Michael Thomas was already assured of a place in Liverpool folklore before he signed in December 1991. It was he who scored Arsenal's famous winner at Anfield to clinch the 1988–89 Championship. Thomas endeared himself to his new fans by scoring in the 1992 FA Cup Final.

U The biggest upset Liverpool have suffered in the FA Cup was a 2–1 defeat by Worcester City in January 1959.

V Harman Van Den Berg was the last of the inter-war South Africans to join Liverpool, signing in October 1937.

W Brothers Walter and Harold Wadsworth were both on the books in the 1920s. The elder Walter, known as 'Big Waddy', played 240 matches to his brother's 54 and was an important part of the side which won the League in 1922 and 1923.

X Liverpool last played on Xmas day in 1958, losing a Second Division fixture 3–1 at Grimsby.

Y Ron Yeats was, in 1965, the first Reds captain to receive the FA Cup.

Z Bruce Grobbelaar is the only Liverpool player to have ever played international football for Zimbabwe.

THROUGH THE YEARS
SEPTEMBER

1884

September

28

September has been a month of firsts for the club and its stadium. Anfield staged its debut competitive fixture in 1884 when Everton beat Earlstown 5-0.

1892

September

1

Liverpool's first game followed eight years later when Rotherham Town visited for a friendly and were thrashed 7-1. Two days after that, Liverpool played their first Lancashire League match, dispatching Higher Walton 8-0, and twelve months on came the first Football League match, Lincoln City on the receiving end of a 4-0 scoreline on 9 September 1893.

1981

September

29

September was also the month when Bill Shankly died, passing away in 1981. The whole city of Liverpool was stunned by the news, and the scale of the tributes was enormous.

1974
September
17

Liverpool's record European win saw Norwegian side Stromsgodset beaten 11-0 in the Cup Winners' Cup.

1989
September
12

Liverpool beat Crystal Palace 9-0. The goals came from Steve Nicol twice, Glenn Hysen, Peter Beardsley, Gary Gillespie, Ian Rush, John Barnes, Steve McMahon and John Aldridge. It equalled Liverpool's biggest margin of victory in a League match.

1986
September

Liverpool won the Screen Sport Super Cup, the only team ever to claim the trophy. It was devised as a competition for the clubs which would have played in Europe in 1985-86, with Liverpool and Everton winning through to contest the Final the following season. Liverpool won the first leg 3-1 on the 16th at Anfield and the second leg 4-1 at Goodison a fortnight later, with Ian Rush scoring five goals over the two games.

BOGEY TEAMS

While Liverpool have beaten Europe's best over the years, two 'unfashionable' sides in England have caused them problems.

Wimbledon and Leicester have both had some sort of hold over the Anfield side in crucial games over the years, with the 1988 FA Cup Final standing head and shoulders above any other match. Overwhelming favourites, Liverpool were expected to just turn up and claim the Cup against first-time Finalists Wimbledon – even though the Dons were also in the First Division – as they had just claimed their 17th League Championship title by nine points.

The pundits were proved wrong, however, as Lawrie Sanchez's first-half header put the south Londoners ahead. Then John Aldridge became the first man to miss a penalty in a Wembley Final when Dave Beasant pushed away his second half spot-kick.

In the 1996–97 season Liverpool lost a rearranged Premiership game 2-1 at Wimbledon, and this, coupled with Newcastle's goalless draw at West Ham on the same night, handed the title to Manchester United.

The Dons also won 2-1 on their first-ever visit to Anfield, knocking Liverpool off the top of the League in the process and only lost three of their first 11 top flight games there. Although the Reds do have a good League record against Wimbledon in London, the Dons knocked them out of the 1993-94 Coca-Cola Cup 4-3 on penalties at Selhurst Park in Round Four.

Leicester held sway over Liverpool at the start of the 1960s, winning five of the sides' first six League meetings after the

Reds returned to the top flight in 1962. In that spell Leicester also beat Liverpool in the 1963 FA Cup Semi-Final, thanks to an inspirational display from England goalkeeper Gordon Banks, before Liverpool finally turned the tables in the 1965 Quarter-Final, winning 1-0 at Anfield after a goalless draw.

However Leicester still had another trick up their sleeve for the future and produced it in January 1981 with a 1-0 League win at Anfield that ended Liverpool's club record 85-match unbeaten home run.

Brighton are another team who have caused Liverpool problems in Cup competitions and beat them in successive seasons in the FA Cup in the early 1980s. The season the Seagulls reached the Final, 1982-83, they pulled off a shock 2-1 win at Anfield in the Fifth Round, one goal coming from former Liverpool hero Jimmy Case, while the following year the Reds lost 2-0 at the Goldstone in Round Four.

While Liverpool have at least beaten Brighton in other years, they have never managed to get past either Huddersfield or Cardiff in the FA Cup. The Terriers claim three wins from their three meetings, with the first a 2-1 win at Leeds Road in 1920 when they were a division below Liverpool. The other two ties were both Fifth Round meetings at Anfield with Huddersfield winning 1-0 in 1938 and 2-0 in 1955.

Cardiff also boast a 100 per cent FA Cup record against Liverpool. The Welsh club were the holders and one of the country's top sides when they first met at Ninian Park in the Fourth Round in 1928 so it was no surprise when the Reds lost 2-1. Two seasons later, Cardiff had been relegated but still managed to pull off a 2-1 Third Round triumph at Anfield.

Surprisingly Liverpool have suffered some embarrassing Cup exits over the years with the 2-1 Third Round defeat at Southern League Worcester City in 1959 and Third Division (North) Gateshead's 1-0 win over them at the same stage six years earlier topping the list.

LEAGUE RECORD

While Liverpool's last Championship was in 1989–90, they do hold the record of 18 title wins.

Season	Division	P	W	D	L	F–A	Pts	Pos
1893–94	Two	28	22	6	—	77–18	50	1st
★ Division Two Champions ★								
1894–95	One	30	7	8	15	51–70	22	16th
Relegated								
1895–96	Two	30	22	2	6	106–32	46	1st
★ Division Two Champions ★								
1896–97	One	30	12	9	9	46–38	33	5th
1897–98	One	30	11	6	13	48–45	28	9th
1898–99	One	34	19	5	10	49–33	43	2nd
● Division One Runners–up ●								
1899–1900	One	34	14	5	15	49–45	33	10th
1900–01	One	34	19	7	8	59–35	45	1st
★ Division One Champions ★								
1901–02	One	34	10	12	12	42–38	32	11th
1902–03	One	34	17	4	13	68–49	38	5th
1903–04	One	34	9	8	17	49–62	26	17th
Relegated								

Season	Division	P	W	D	L	F-A	Pts	Pos
1904-05	Two	34	27	4	3	93-25	58	1st
★ Division Two Champions ★								
1905-06	One	38	23	5	10	79-46	51	1st
★ Division One Champions ★								
1906-07	One	38	13	7	18	64-65	33	15th
1907-08	One	38	16	6	16	68-61	38	8th
1908-09	One	38	15	6	17	57-65	36	16th
1909-10	One	38	21	6	11	78-57	48	2nd
● Division One Runners-up ●								
1910-11	One	38	15	7	16	53-53	37	13th
1911-12	One	38	12	10	16	49-55	34	17th
1912-13	One	38	16	5	17	61-71	37	12th
1913-14	One	38	14	7	17	46-62	35	16th
1914-15	One	38	14	9	15	65-75	37	14th
1919-20	One	42	19	10	13	59-44	48	4th
1920-21	One	42	18	15	9	63-35	51	4th
1921-22	One	42	22	13	7	63-36	57	1st
★ Division One Champions ★								
1922-23	One	42	26	8	8	70-31	60	1st
★ Division One Champions ★								
1923-24	One	42	15	11	16	49-48	41	12th
1924-25	One	42	20	10	12	63-55	50	4th
1925-26	One	42	14	16	12	70-63	44	7th
1926-27	One	42	18	7	17	69-61	43	9th
1927-28	One	42	13	13	16	84-87	39	16th
1928-29	One	42	17	12	13	90-64	46	5th
1929-30	One	42	16	9	17	63-79	41	12th
1930-31	One	42	15	12	15	86-85	42	9th
1931-32	One	42	19	6	17	81-93	44	10th

LIVERPOOL

Season	Division	P	W	D	L	F-A	Pts	Pos
1932-33	One	42	14	11	17	79-84	39	14th
1933-34	One	42	14	10	18	79-87	38	18th
1934-35	One	42	19	7	16	85-88	45	7th
1935-36	One	42	13	12	17	60-64	38	19th
1936-37	One	42	12	11	19	62-84	35	18th
1937-38	One	42	15	11	16	65-71	41	11th
1938-39	One	42	14	14	14	62-63	42	11th
1946-47	One	42	25	7	10	84-52	57	1st
★ Division One Champions ★								
1947-48	One	42	16	10	16	65-61	42	11th
1948-49	One	42	13	14	15	53-43	40	12th
1949-50	One	42	17	14	11	64-54	48	8th
1950-51	One	42	16	11	15	53-59	43	9th
1951-52	One	42	12	19	11	57-61	43	11th
1952-53	One	42	14	8	20	61-82	36	17th
1953-54	One	42	9	10	23	68-97	28	22nd
Relegated								
1954-55	Two	42	16	10	16	92-96	42	11th
1955-56	Two	42	21	6	15	85-63	48	3rd
1956-57	Two	42	21	11	10	82-54	53	3rd
1957-58	Two	42	22	10	10	79-54	54	4th
1958-59	Two	42	24	5	13	87-62	53	4th
1959-60	Two	42	20	10	12	90-66	50	3rd
1960-61	Two	42	21	10	11	87-58	52	3rd
1961-62	Two	42	27	8	7	99-43	62	1st
★ Division Two Champions ★								
1962-63	One	42	17	10	15	71-59	44	8th
1963-64	One	42	26	5	11	92-45	57	1st
★ Division One Champions ★								
1964-65	One	42	17	10	15	67-73	44	7th

Season	Division	P	W	D	L	F-A	Pts	Pos
1965-66	One	42	26	9	7	79-34	61	1st
★ Division One Champions ★								
1966-67	One	42	19	13	10	64-47	51	5th
1967-68	One	42	22	11	9	71-40	55	3rd
1968-69	One	42	25	11	6	63-24	61	2nd
● Division One Runners-up ●								
1969-70	One	42	20	11	11	65-42	51	5th
1970-71	One	42	17	17	8	42-24	51	5th
1971-72	One	42	24	9	9	64-30	57	3rd
1972-73	One	42	25	10	7	72-42	60	1st
★ Division One Champions ★								
1973-74	One	42	22	13	7	52-31	57	2nd
● Division One Runners-up ●								
1974-75	One	42	20	11	11	60-39	51	2nd
● Division One Runners-up ●								
1975-76	One	42	23	14	5	66-31	60	1st
★ Division One Champions ★								
1976-77	One	42	23	11	8	62-33	57	1st
★ Division One Champions ★								
1977-78	One	42	24	9	9	65-34	57	2nd
● Division One Runners-up ●								
1978-79	One	42	30	8	4	85-16	68	1st
★ Division One Champions ★								

LIVERPOOL

Season	Division	P	W	D	L	F-A	Pts	Pos
1979–80	One	42	25	10	7	81-30	60	1st

⭐ **Division One Champions** ⭐

Season	Division	P	W	D	L	F-A	Pts	Pos
1980–81	One	42	17	17	8	62-42	51	5th
1981–82	One	42	26	9	7	80-32	87	1st

⭐ **Division One Champions** ⭐

1982–83	One	42	24	10	8	87-37	82	1st

⭐ **Division One Champions** ⭐

1983–84	One	42	22	14	6	73-32	80	1st

⭐ **Division One Champions** ⭐

1984–85	One	42	22	11	9	68-35	77	2nd

● **Division One Runners-up** ●

1985–86	One	42	26	10	6	89-37	88	1st

⭐ **Division One Champions** ⭐

1986–87	One	42	23	8	11	72-42	77	2nd

● **Division One Runners-up** ●

1987–88	One	40	26	12	2	87-24	90	1st

⭐ **Division One Champions** ⭐

1988–89	One	38	22	10	6	65-28	76	2nd

● **Division One Runners-up** ●

1989–90	One	38	23	10	5	78-37	79	1st

⭐ **Division One Champions** ⭐

1990–91	One	38	23	7	8	77-40	76	2nd

● **Division One Runners-up** ●

Season	Division	P	W	D	L	F-A	Pts	Pos
1991-92	One	42	16	16	10	47-40	64	6th
1992-93	Premier	42	16	11	15	62-55	59	6th
1993-94	Premier	42	17	9	16	59-55	60	8th
1994-95	Premier	42	21	11	10	65-37	74	4th
1995-96	Premier	38	20	11	7	70-34	71	3rd
1996-97	Premier	38	19	11	8	62-37	68	4th

THROUGH THE YEARS
OCTOBER

1894

October

13

The first League encounter between Liverpool and Everton took place. Liverpool went away for a week's training before the match, but it did them little good: they went down 3-0 in front of 44,000 people, including an array of Liverpool city dignitaries.

1957

October

30

Anfield's floodlights were first used as Liverpool and Everton played a friendly. The lights cost £12,000 to erect, while Liverpool won the match 3-2. It was an era when there were few matches between the two rivals because they were in different divisions.

1974

October

Phil Neal became Bob Paisley's first signing for Liverpool, joining for £60,000 from Northampton Town.

1977
October
12

50,000 people saw Scotland beat Wales 2-0 at Anfield to qualify for the 1978 World Cup Finals.

1983
October
29

Ian Rush scored five goals in a League match for the only time in his career, helping Liverpool to a 6-0 victory over Luton Town.

1993
October
5

Robbie Fowler repeated the trick, scoring five times against Fulham in the Second Round, second leg of the League Cup, Liverpool winning 5-0.

1987
October
18

Ray Houghton signed for Liverpool, adding to earlier arrivals John Barnes and Peter Beardsley. Together with another recent signing, John Aldridge, the players helped Liverpool to some dazzling displays as they won the Championship with just two defeats.

KEEPERS KORNER

Legendary Liverpool manager Bill Shankly used to build his teams straight down the middle – a goalkeeper, centre-half and centre-forward were his main priorities, believing you could build round such a solid backbone. And the search for glory, naturally, started with the Number 1 shirt.

 ## ELISHA SCOTT

L iverpool have a long tradition of fine goalkeepers, and one of the first to make a lasting impression was Elisha Scott. Signed in 1912 from Belfast Celtic, he made his debut at the beginning of the following year, and once established was to play 467 games in the League and FA Cup for the Reds until he left in 1934.

Scott was noted for having what contemporary reporters noted as 'the eye of an eagle' and 'the swift movement of a panther', the latter description all the more admirable as he always dressed in two pairs of socks and three sweaters for each match! But it was his ability to keep Liverpool's goals against tally down that was of most value. In the Championship season of 1921-22 Liverpool conceded just 36 goals, and when they won the title again 12 months later the total was down to 31.

Scott's rivalry with Everton striker Dixie Dean was highlighted during the Merseyside derbies of the 1920s, with the games being previewed as a clash between the two. At one stage Everton tried to sign Scott for £250 but were turned down after Liverpool fans wrote to the club in numbers to protest.

Scott made his Irish international debut in 1920, and won 31 caps altogether, 27 while with Liverpool. When he left the Reds, it was to return to to his native city to play for and manage Belfast Celtic. He stopped playing in 1936 but remained as manager until the club folded in 1949. Scott died in May 1959 at the age of 64.

ELISHA SCOTT LIVERPOOL APPS 1912-34				
League	FA Cup	League Cup	Europe	Total
430	37	—	—	467

 # TOMMY LAWRENCE

He may not conform to the slimline profile of today's goalkeeper, but it wasn't just the bulk of Tommy Lawrence that made him difficult to beat. The 'Flying Pig', as the Kop affectionately dubbed him, proved an important third of the backbone of Bill Shankly's successful 1960s side, built as it was down the middle with fellow Scots Ron Yeats at centre-half and Ian St John at centre-forward.

A five-year apprenticeship came to an end when Jim Furnell injured a finger and found Lawrence impossible to displace thereafter. The next seven and a half seasons would see him miss just five games, as well as picking up League Championship and FA Cup medals as Shankly's Liverpool wrote their name large on the footballing map. Ever alert to danger, Lawrence would race from his area in the manner Bruce Grobbelaar would later turn into a trademark.

Lawrence and his defence conceded just 24 goals in season 1968-69, thereby establishing a League record, and it begs the question of why he was only capped three times for his country. (Perhaps it was because Tommy, who joined the club after youth trials, never played Scottish League football.) But injury in 1970 gave understudy Ray Clemence a chance to stake his claim and, in the face of competition from the future England international, Lawrence took the ferry cross the Mersey to Prenton Park. A further 80 games followed before he hung up his gloves, but there was no doubt that Tommy Lawrence's heart belonged to Anfield.

TOMMY LAWRENCE LIVERPOOL APPS 1962-71				
League	FA Cup	League Cup	Europe	Total
306	42	6	33	387

 # RAY CLEMENCE

With Liverpool dominating English football in the 1970s and 1980s, a reliable goalkeeper was vital. Ray Clemence, signed from Scunthorpe United for £18,000 in June 1967, fitted the bill. He made his debut in the 1969-70 season and by the end of the campaign he had ousted Tommy Lawrence, who had been in Liverpool's goal for eight highly successful years.

A masterful goalkeeper with a full range of skills, Clemence was to contribute in substantial amounts to more than a decade of success. He was to win five Championships, three European Cups, two UEFA Cups, one FA Cup and one League Cup. He was reliable and made meaningful saves at crucial moments, such as from Stielike in the 1977 European Cup Final when the scores were locked at 1-1.

His finest season was the Championship year of 1978-79, when Liverpool conceded just 16 goals in a campaign lasting

42 games. Clemence recorded a staggering 28 clean sheets. They also didn't concede a goal in the FA Cup until being beaten by Manchester United in the Semi-Final.

It came as a major surprise when Clemence decided to leave in the summer of 1981, moving to Tottenham Hotspur for £300,000. Still at the top of his game, he won more honours with Spurs and added to the 59 England caps he had gained while with the Reds, a figure that would surely have been higher had he not been in competition with Peter Shilton for the right to be regarded as England's finest. Ironically his first season with Spurs saw his new side coming face to face with his old in the League Cup Final at Wembley, and Spurs were within two minutes of victory when Clemence was beaten by Ronnie Whelan, Liverpool triumphing in extra time.

Clemence played a total of 656 matches with Liverpool, and after retiring from playing, he managed Spurs in tandem with Doug Livermore and then had a period in charge of Barnet.

RAY CLEMENCE LIVERPOOL APPS 1968-81				
League	FA Cup	League Cup	Europe	Total
470	54	55	77	656

 # BRUCE GROBBELAAR

The void left by Clemence was more than ably filled by Bruce Grobbelaar. Signed from Vancouver Whitecaps for £250,000 in March 1981, the South African-born Zimbabwe international had spent the 1979-80 season with Crewe Alexandra.

One of the game's great eccentrics and noted for his ability to sprint from his area in order to clear up danger, Grobbelaar's occasional costly errors should not disguise what an able and committed goalkeeper he was. His performance in the 1986 FA Cup Final against Everton was particularly memorable, with Grobbelaar producing an outstanding fingertip save from Graeme Sharp's header as well as almost fighting with team-mate Jim Beglin as he vented his anger at what was going on in front of him.

Also unforgettable was his performance in helping Liverpool to their fourth European Cup. The match with Roma went to a penalty shoot-out, and with the score at 3-2 to Liverpool, Italian international Graziani lined up Roma's fourth kick. To everyone's astonishment, Grobbelaar indulged in some clowning activities, feigning nervousness and wobbling his knees, and Graziani duly skied his kick over the bar, leaving Alan Kennedy to wrap up the Cup for the Reds.

Grobbelaar didn't miss a match during his first five seasons as a first-team regular but was out of the team for a while in the 1988-89 season with meningitis. The arrival of David James seemed to spell the end for Grobbelaar, but he remained with the club until a free transfer took him to Southampton for the 1994-95 season. He played 579 times for Liverpool and won six Championships, three FA Cups, three League Cups and the European Cup.

A cloud was put over his Anfield career when he was accused of involvement in match-fixing. Two Liverpool matches were highlighted, a 3-3 draw at home to Manchester United and a 3-0 defeat at Newcastle. After two court hearings, Grobbelaar's good name was restored when he was cleared of the charges.

BRUCE GROBBELAAR LIVERPOOL APPS 1981-94				
League	FA Cup	League Cup	Europe	Total
440	62	70	7	579

DAVID JAMES

The latest last line of defence for Liverpool is David James, a highly talented keeper but one who has suffered the occasional loss of form. Signed for £1.3 million from Watford in July 1992, James made his debut on the opening day of the season at Sheffield United. However, he lost his place after just 11 games and was not recalled until January 1993. He kept his first clean sheet at the end of that month, a single-goal victory at Arsenal.

However, he lost confidence and was reserve to Bruce Grobbelaar by the time the 1993-94 season began. He might even have left Anfield, offered as part-exchange in a bid to bring Blackburn's Tim Flowers to the club.

It was Roy Evans who was to revitalise James' Anfield career, bringing him back into the team when he was appointed manager and then releasing Grobbelaar, confirming James as his top goalkeeper. The player responded by becoming a custodian in the Anfield tradition, and was voted into the PFA Premiership representative team in 1996. He was finally given international recognition at the start of the 1996-97 campaign and made his debut in a friendly against Mexico in March 1997. The signing of American Brad Friedel in late 1997 once again put James under pressure, but it seemed certain that David James had already written himself into the Anfield story.

DAVID JAMES LIVERPOOL APPS 1991-(97)				
League	FA Cup	League Cup	Europe	Total
161	16	17	13	207

BEST SEASON 3

Despite enormous success in the 1960s, 1970s and 1980s, Liverpool's only League title this decade to date was won in 1989-90. Here's how it happened.

Always setting their sights high, the Reds were even more determined to succeed this time round, having lost the Championship at the very end of the previous season to Arsenal at Anfield. Stylish Swedish defender Glenn Hysen from Fiorentina was the only major arrival, while Kevin MacDonald and Jim Beglin left the club.

Liverpool started with two wins and two draws before newly-promoted Crystal Palace came to Anfield and were trounced 9-0. The Reds hit the top at the end of September with a 3-1 victory over Everton and remained there despite a 4-1 defeat at Southampton. Other defeats followed, Coventry winning 1-0 at Anfield and QPR 3-2 at Loftus Road, while the Reds' fourth League defeat of the season was not long in coming – 2-0 at Sheffield Wednesday on the club's first visit to Hillsborough since the events of the previous April.

However, Liverpool were to lose just once more in the League as they got into gear and simply stormed to the title. They led the table by four points from Aston Villa at the end of 1989, but Villa had come back to lead the table in March. Liverpool regained the leadership at the end of the month, despite losing 1-0 at Tottenham.

The arrival of Ronnie Rosenthal on loan from Standard Liege proved to be the catalyst for Liverpool's title run-in. Employed initially as a 'supersub', the Israeli international scored some vital goals and worried opposing defences with his all-action style, striking a hat-trick in his first full match against Charlton.

Liverpool needed four points from their last three matches to clinch the title, but their 2-1 victory over QPR coupled with Villa's 3-3 draw with Norwich gave them their 18th Championship, the 1-0 victory over Derby and the 6-1 revenge visit to Coventry mere formalities. They scored 78 League goals and 106 in total, with John Barnes leading the way with 28 goals. Ian Rush managed 26 as he fully re-established himself in the side after his Italian 'holiday'.

There was disappointment in the FA Cup, however, with Liverpool losing 4-3 to Crystal Palace in an epic encounter when, for the first time ever, the Semi-Finals were shown live on television one after the other. The outcome was sweet revenge for Palace after their heavy defeat at Anfield, and the only blot on Liverpool's memorable campaign.

1989-90 LEAGUE RECORD

Opponents	Home	Away
Arsenal	2-1	1-1
Aston Villa	1-1	1-1
Charlton Athletic	1-0	4-0
Chelsea	4-1	5-2
Coventry City	0-1	6-1
Crystal Palace	9-0	2-0
Derby County	1-0	3-0
Everton	2-1	3-1
Luton Town	2-2	0-0
Manchester City	3-1	4-1
Manchester United	0-0	2-1
Millwall	1-0	2-1
Norwich City	0-0	0-0
Nottingham Forest	2-2	2-2
Queens Park Rangers	2-1	2-3
Sheffield Wednesday	2-1	0-2
Southampton	3-2	1-4
Tottenham Hotspur	1-0	0-1
Wimbledon	2-1	2-1

THROUGH THE YEARS
NOVEMBER

1934
November
10

Liverpool suffered their worst ever League defeat when they lost 8-0 at Huddersfield's Leeds Road ground.

1959
November
12

Phil Taylor resigned as Liverpool manager. The captain of Liverpool's Cup Final team of 1950, he was the only Liverpool manager not to be in charge of the side in the top division, being unable to take them up despite never finishing lower than fourth in the table. The final straw for the Liverpool management was a 5-4 defeat at Swansea.

1969
November
15

Football coverage on television had been in black and white until today, when a colour transmission of Liverpool's home encounter with West Ham United was broadcast.

1982
November
6

Ian Rush scored four times at Everton as Liverpool recorded a memorable 5-0 derby victory.

1988
November
30

The club suffered their worst League Cup defeat at West Ham, crashing to a surprising 4-1 loss.

1995
November

Liverpool suffered one of their worst ever months when they failed to win a single game, the period coming to be known as 'Black November'. They lost 2-1 at Newcastle, 2-1 at home to Everton, 2-1 at Middlesbrough and 1-0 at home to Newcastle in the Coca-Cola Cup, with a goalless draw at West Ham the only thing to show for their efforts.

GREAT DEFENDERS

Much of Liverpool's success over the years has been built on solid defending, and the captain of the club has often been a figure from the heart of the defence. Ever since towering Scot Ron Yeats led the Reds back into the First Division in 1962 and then became the first Liverpool skipper to lift the FA Cup, defensive players have featured prominently in the history of the club.

 ## TOMMY SMITH

Manager Bill Shankly wanted a hard man – and that's what he got after spotting the potential in 15-year-old Tommy Smith when signing him in 1962.

Liverpool-born Smith was an uncompromising defender who had opponents quaking in their boots even before kick-off, but the self-confessed 'headcase' had a steep learning curve at Liverpool after making his debut at 17. This was wonderfully illustrated in his first match against Manchester United at Anfield when experienced Scot Denis Law, annoyed at the unrelenting attention he was getting, feigned a headbutt. The Kop jeered Smith's over-reaction, leaving him humiliated.

He grew up fast and became part of a formidable unit alongside Ron Yeats before taking the central-defensive role himself. Dubbed the 'Anfield Iron', Smith was sent off just once in his career which underlined his 'hard but fair' attitude to the game. He'd play most of his later games at Anfield in the Number 2 shirt, having moved over to make way for Hughes and Thompson.

Smith's finest moment at Liverpool was one of his last at the club. After regaining a place in the side through injury, he made his 600th appearance for Liverpool in the 1977 European Cup Final against Moenchengladbach and scored a rare goal with a bullet header from the edge of the box to put Liverpool on the path to a 3-1 victory. He should have made the Final the following year but, after dropping an axe on his foot while gardening, was forced onto the sidelines.

He left the club in 1978 to join John Toshack's Swansea and currently commentates for Merseyside's local radio.

TOMMY SMITH LIVERPOOL RECORD 1963-78

League		FA Cup		League Cup		Europe		Total	
Apps	Goals	Apps	Goals	Apps	Goals	Apps	Goals	Apps	Goals
467	36	52	2	30	2	84	8	633	48

 # EMLYN HUGHES

Emlyn Hughes was still a teenager when Bill Shankly bought him from Blackpool for a then record fee of £65,000 in February 1967. A player of tremendous enthusiasm and energy and later an inspirational captain, Hughes made his debut at home to Stoke City a month after signing, initially operating on the left of midfield in the Number 6 shirt. He'd soon move back to play central defence and, occasionally, full-back in the coming decade.

At first Hughes was part of a young, evolving Liverpool side, with the players who had won promotion from the

Second Division, as well as two League Championships and the FA Cup, gradually making way for the new stars that Shankly was introducing. However, it wasn't long before this new Liverpool team started winning trophies, and Hughes was to pick up four Championships, two European Cups – making him the first Liverpool captain to lift that trophy – two UEFA cups and the FA Cup.

Although known as 'Crazy Horse', he brought calm to his defence during his 657 games for the club in which he notched 48 goals. Captain of England as well, he played 59 times for the national side while at Anfield.

He left Liverpool for Wolves in the summer of 1979 and promptly filled the only gap in his medal collection by winning the League Cup. When he retired from playing, he went into management, though not with great success, but eventually found his niche on television, particularly on the quiz show *A Question Of Sport*.

EMLYN HUGHES LIVERPOOL RECORD 1967-79

League		FA Cup		League Cup		Europe		Total	
Apps	Goals	Apps	Goals	Apps	Goals	Apps	Goals	Apps	Goals
474	35	62	1	46	3	75	9	657	48

PHIL NEAL

Bob Paisley's first move into the transfer market could not have been more inspired. In October 1974 he spent £60,000 to bring Northampton defender Phil Neal to Anfield. A talented full-back with a penchant for overlapping runs and creating goals, Neal hardly missed a match during his Anfield career.

He was also the club's penalty taker, scoring from many vital spot-kicks, not least the clinching third goal in the club's first European Cup Final success against Borussia Moenchengladbach in 1977. Neal scored in the 1984 Final against Roma as well – but unusually this was from open play, giving Liverpool an early lead in a game which finished 1-1. He then converted one of the penalties in the subsequent shoot-out, the first Liverpool scored having gone 1-0 down after the first two kicks.

He was the highest medal winner in the history of English football and shared the Liverpool record of seven Championship successes with Phil Thompson when he left the club, although those records were soon to be broken. In addition he was the only player to appear in all four successful European Cup Finals and won four League Cups and the UEFA Cup. The FA Cup was the only medal he missed out on, and he had a single runners-up medal to show for the competition. He took over the club captaincy when Graeme Souness left for Sampdoria, but unfortunately for him he became the only Liverpool captain of that era not to lift a trophy. He also won 50 England caps.

He had played 635 games scoring 60 goals by the time he left Anfield in November 1985 to become player-manager at Bolton. He has had a mixed managerial career, including assisting Graham Taylor when he was the England manager in the 1990s.

PHIL NEAL LIVERPOOL RECORD 1974-85									
League		FA Cup		League Cup		Europe		Total	
Apps	Goals	Apps	Goals	Apps	Goals	Apps	Goals	Apps	Goals
455	41	66	4	45	3	69	12	635	60

ALAN HANSEN

Neal was unlucky in the timing of his departure, in that Liverpool went on to complete their historic double at the end of the 1985-86 season, and the honour of lifting the trophies went to centre-half Alan Hansen. Signed from Partick Thistle for £100,000 in April 1977, he took a year or so to become fully established in the team. A calm and assured defender who had the skill to set up a number of attacking moves, he was one of the most formidable central defenders in Europe when at his peak, which makes his tally of just 26 Scotland caps all the more remarkable. He was surprisingly omitted from the party for the 1986 World Cup Finals.

Injured before the 1988-89 season, Hansen returned to claim his second FA Cup winner's medal. He would also top Phil Neal by claiming eight Championships, as well as four League and three European Cups. An intelligent and articulate man, Hansen was widely tipped to move into Liverpool's coaching set-up. However, he announced his retirement just a week after Kenny Dalglish quit as manager in a move to dampen the speculation that was already springing up about his succeeding his fellow Scot.

Hansen played 607 matches for Liverpool scoring 13 times. Since retiring he has become a well-respected expert summariser of the game with the BBC.

ALAN HANSEN LIVERPOOL RECORD 1977-91									
League		FA Cup		League Cup		Europe		Total	
Apps	Goals	Apps	Goals	Apps	Goals	Apps	Goals	Apps	Goals
436	7	60	2	68	1	43	3	607	13

MARK WRIGHT

There is no doubt that on his day, Mark Wright is a defender to compare with the best of his breed. However, inconsistent form and a series of injuries have seen him in and out of the Liverpool side.

Signed for £2.2 million from Derby in July 1991 – Graeme Souness' first signing and a then record fee for a defender – Wright made his debut against Oldham alongside fellow Derby refugee Dean Saunders. However, he was injured within two games and was out for three months. He was rewarded on his return with the captaincy and lifted the FA Cup against Sunderland a few months later.

However injury kept him out of the side for much of the next two years, and when John Scales and Phil Babb arrived at the club, Wright's days at Anfield seemed over.

Nevertheless, he emerged from the reserves in March 1995 to give an acclaimed performance in a 2-0 Anfield victory over Manchester United, and he was given the chance to re-establish himself at the beginning of the 1995-96 season, which he grasped. The forgotten man of English football enjoyed a renaissance which would have included a place in England's Euro '96 squad had an injury not prevented him from taking his place.

He remained a dependable figure at the back throughout the following season bringing his total Liverpool matches over the 200 mark and has finally started to show the calm assurance and reliability that he displayed at Oxford, Southampton and Derby.

MARK WRIGHT LIVERPOOL RECORD 1991-(97)									
League		FA Cup		League Cup		Europe		Total	
Apps	Goals	Apps	Goals	Apps	Goals	Apps	Goals	Apps	Goals
152	5	18	—	16	2	16	2	202	9

THE WAR YEARS

When the Football League was suspended in September 1939, Liverpool were fourth in the First Division after their opening three matches.

The League programme was scrapped and after a series of friendly matches were played, regional matches were organised. Liverpool spent their revised 1939-40 campaign in the West League with clubs as diverse as the two Manchester sides, Everton and Port Vale. Stoke won the 22-game season, finishing ahead of Liverpool by two points.

The following campaign, the teams were split into north and south regions with the Champions decided by goal average. Sides were allowed to choose their own opponents, with the only proviso being that First and Second Division clubs had to play at least two Third Division sides. Liverpool finished 16th out of 36 sides in the strange-looking table, having played 37 matches.

The North Championship in 1941-42 involved 38 teams, but this time each side played 18 matches, nine at home and nine away, with positions again being decided on points. Blackpool took the pre-Christmas title with Liverpool eighth. In the New Year there was a second campaign which saw the Reds finish fourth behind Manchester United.

The 1942-43 season saw Liverpool lift their only wartime trophy when they won the second North Championship of the season, finishing five points ahead of Lovell's Athletic, Manchester City and Aston Villa. They were runners-up to Blackpool in the pre-Christmas League.

In 1943-44 Liverpool came third in both North Championships, with Bath bizarrely winning the second one, and 1944-45 saw them third again in the second League and 16th in the first. The final wartime League season saw smaller full season leagues with the Anfield side 11th in the North League in which Sheffield United claimed the title.

Liverpool made little impact in any of the Wartime Cup competitions, only reaching the last eight once, in the 1944-45 League North Cup, and suffering defeats by Barrow and Southport in earlier successive seasons. Their only highlight was an 8-1 hammering of Oldham in 1943-44.

One of the highspots for Merseyside fans meanwhile was the continuation of the derby matches with Everton. Liverpool enjoyed the better results, though Everton knocked them out of the 1941-42 League Cup, and the supporters turned up in their droves. The Toffees' three best wartime attendances were not surprisingly against their rivals from across Stanley Park. The best of these was the 60,926 gathering who watched a 2-2 draw in 1945-46.

With many of the country's players serving their country, clubs used guest players for matches. Liverpool were no different to any other side in this respect, but did get into trouble for playing Peter Docherty in a match at Blackpool in 1941-42 after the Manchester City star had just turned up to watch the game. He replaced George Ainsley, who had been given permission by the RAF to play, and the Air Force initially refused to lend the Anfield side any more players.

Other players who guested for Liverpool during the hostilities included Frank Swift, Sam Bartram, Stan Cullis, Johnny Carey and a certain Bill Shankly.

Football during the First World War was not as well-organised. The 1914-15 season was completed, with Liverpool 13th in Division One, before the game was split up into regional divisions. The Lancashire section title came to Anfield in 1916-17 and League football resumed in 1919-20.

GAFFERSPEAK

Anfield's bosses have rarely been short of wit or wisdom. Here's a selection of choice quotes and quips from the bootroom.

'Football is a simple game based on the giving and taking of passes, of controlling the ball and of making yourself available to receive a pass. It is terribly simple.'   *Bill Shankly*

'If a player is not interfering with play or seeking to gain an advantage, then he should be.'   *Bill Shankly*

'If you are first you are first. If you are second, you are nothing.'   *Bill Shankly*

'He typifies everything that is good in football, and he has never changed. You could stake your life on Ian.'
Bill Shankly on Ian Callaghan

'Yes, Roger Hunt misses a few, but he gets in the right place to miss them.'   *Bill Shankly*

'With him in defence, we could play Arthur Askey in goal.'
Bill Shankly after signing Ron Yeats

'If Everton were playing at the bottom of the garden, I'd pull the curtains.'   *Bill Shankly*

'You, son – you could start a riot in a graveyard.'
Bill Shankly to Tommy Smith

'Take that bandage off. And what do you mean about *your* knee? It's Liverpool's knee!'

> *Bill Shankly to Tommy Smith, who was trying to explain that he was injured because he had a bandage on his knee*

'Son, you'll do well here as long as you remember two things. Don't over-eat and don't lose your accent.'

> *Bill Shankly on signing fellow Scot Ian St John*

'Still we've had the hard times, too – one year we finished second.'

> *Bob Paisley*

'If you're in the penalty area and don't know what to do with the ball, put it in the net and we'll discuss the options later.'

> *Bob Paisley*

'Bill was so strong it was unbelievable. You couldn't shake him off the ball. It didn't matter where he was playing, though I suppose his best position was outside-left. He could go round you, or past you, or even straight through you sometimes!'

> *Bob Paisley on Billy Liddell*

'He's not coming out. He says he wouldn't know what to say.'

> *Graeme Souness on Robbie Fowler's five-goal haul against Fulham in September 1993*

'He's better than Brian Lara because he's 600 not out. What a guy.'

> *Roy Evans marking Ian Rush's 600th appearance for Liverpool*

'If I'd agreed to pay a 21-year-old who hadn't played for England £12,000, I would have had 10 guys knocking on my door saying they were full internationals and that they wanted the same money.'

> *Roy Evans when asked why he didn't buy Chris Sutton, 1994*

THROUGH THE YEARS
DECEMBER

1915
December
23

The results of the inquiry into the Liverpool and Manchester United betting scandal of 1915 were announced at the end of that year. Four players from each side were found guilty of colluding to fix the Old Trafford fixture between the clubs which had been played on Good Friday. United won the game 2-0. The Liverpool players banned had their suspensions lifted after the First World War.

1954
December
11

Liverpool equalled their biggest margin of defeat, losing 9-1 at Birmingham City in their first season back in Division Two.

1959
December
1

Bill Shankly was appointed manager of Liverpool. His predecessor Phil Taylor had resigned three weeks before. Shankly, manager of Huddersfield at the time of his appointment, had applied for the post previously when Taylor had been appointed in 1956, but this time was head-hunted. He instituted the famous bootroom at Anfield, having told the existing backroom staff that their positions were safe as soon as he arrived. He also insisted on total freedom from the Liverpool board to pick the side, a change from what had gone before. The results he delivered more than justified his way of doing things.

1966
December
7

Liverpool suffered their worst European defeat, losing 5-1 at Ajax in farcical, fog-bound conditions in the UEFA Cup.

1990
December
15

Steve McManaman first appeared for Liverpool, replacing Peter Beardsley in a League match against Sheffield United. Though he failed to get on the scoresheet the Reds won 2-0.

1996
December
14

Robbie Fowler scored his 100th goal for Liverpool in a 5-1 Anfield demolition of Middlesbrough. Fowler's contribution was four goals, the second being the one which brought up his century.

THE KITBAG

Although strongly associated with their red shirts, Liverpool first played in blue and white quarters, changing to red in time for the 1898-99 campaign.

Their strip was to remain largely unchanged for over 50 years after that, apart from some alterations to the design of the collar. Shorts were white throughout and socks red, though occasionally with hoops. As today, the away kit could be changed depending on the opposition, but white shirts tended to predominate. Shorts were either white or black at first, the latter becoming permanent by the time Liverpool wore them in the 1949-50 FA Cup Final defeat.

Badges only appeared on shirts on special occasions, such as the above-mentioned Cup Final, but became a permanent feature of the strip within a few years, the badge being an oval showing a Liver bird and the letters LFC. The white shorts developed a red trim and socks were hooped red and white.

The next fundamental change came in the 1964-65 season, when Liverpool changed to the now familiar red shorts. The all-red strip made its debut against Anderlecht in the Second Round of the club's inaugural European Cup campaign and was subsequently retained.

Apart from minor collar adjustments, the badge losing the oval to become a little simpler and some yellow trimmings appearing, little changed until 1979, when Liverpool became the first British club to take on a kit sponsorship deal. The name Hitachi began to be displayed on the shirts, but not in all competitions as sponsorship was banned in some cases.

The next major change was in time for the 1982-83 campaign. The shirts had a white pinstripe running down them, and white trim was added to the shorts, while the away strip changed to all yellow with red trim. The shirt sponsor became Crown Paints.

Liverpool then changed manufacturer to Adidas from Umbro, and the new kit was used from the tail end of the 1984-85 campaign. The pinstripes disappeared and instead white stripes were put on the shoulders and the shorts. The away strip reverted to the traditional white shirts and black shorts, but reverted within a season to yellow and red.

For 1987-88 the badge was changed once more, with the bird now sitting proudly in a shield and Liverpool's name spelt out in full. The Adidas white stripes extended down the whole arm. The away strip changed yet again to silver with red trim. In 1988-89 Candy became the sponsor.

For the 1991-92 season, the mirroring white stripes disappeared to leave three bold white lines on the right shoulder and three equally heavy white lines on the left side of the shorts. Away shirts were an identical design, but in a dark green. Carlsberg came in as sponsor in 1992-93 and a Liverpool centenary badge adorned the shirts.

In 1993-94 the thick white stripes migrated downwards and multiplied, so that they were low on both sides of the shirts as well as either side of the shorts. Hoops were added to the socks, while a badge featuring the Shankly Gates and the Hillsborough flame appeared on the shirts. The away kit stayed green but introduced white quarters on the shirts. A third strip of black and gold was introduced. In 1995-96 the white lines thinned while the green strip darkened.

Reebok took over for 1996-97 and the shirts became simpler with much of the trimming removed, though the badge was placed in an oval once again. The away shirt was designated as ecru with black shorts. This became the third strip for 1997-98 when a yellow away kit was brought in.

EUROPEAN CUP

The ultimate club competition has inspired some epic performances from the Reds, winners on four occasions.

Stage	Opponents	Home	Away	Agg
1964-65				
Prelim	KR Reykjavik	6-1	5-0	11-1
Round 1	Anderlecht	3-0	1-0	4-0
Quarter-Final	Cologne	0-0	0-0	0-0
The replay in Rotterdam finished 2-2. Liverpool won on the toss of a coin.				
Semi-Final	Inter Milan	3-1	0-3	3-4
1966-67				
Round 1	Petrolul Ploiesti	2-0	1-3	3-3
Liverpool won the replay in Brussels 2-0.				
Round 2	Ajax	2-2	1-5	3-7
1973-74				
Round 1	Jeunesse D'Esch	2-0	1-1	3-1
Round 2	Red Star Belgrade	1-2	1-2	2-4
1976-77				
Round 1	Crusaders	2-0	5-0	7-0
Round 2	Trabzonspor	3-0	0-1	3-1
Quarter-Final	St Etienne	3-1	0-1	3-2
Semi-Final	Zurich	3-0	3-1	6-1
Final	B Moenchengladbach	—	—	3-1

Stage	Opponents	Home	Away	Agg
	1977-78			
Round 1	Bye	—	—	—
Round 2	Dynamo Dresden	5-1	1-2	6-3
Quarter-Final	Benfica	4-1	2-1	6-2
Semi-Final	B Moenchengladbach	3-0	1-2	4-2
Final	FC Bruges	—	—	1-0
	1978-79			
Round 1	Nottingham Forest	0-0	0-2	0-2
	1979-80			
Round 1	Dinamo Tbilisi	2-1	0-3	2-4
	1980-81			
Round 1	OPS Oulu Palloseura	10-1	1-1	11-2
Round 2	Aberdeen	4-0	1-0	5-0
Quarter-Final	CSKA Sofia	5-1	1-0	6-1
Semi-Final	Bayern Munich	0-0	1-1	1-1
	Liverpool won on away goals.			
Final	Real Madrid	—	—	1-0
	1981-82			
Round 1	OPS Oulu Palloseura	7-0	1-0	8-0
Round 2	AZ 67 Alkmaar	3-2	2-2	5-4
Quarter-Final	CSKA Sofia	1-0	0-2	1-2
	1982-83			
Round 1	Dundalk	1-0	4-1	5-1
Round 2	HJK Helsinki	5-0	0-1	5-1
Quarter-Final	Widzew Lodz	3-2	0-2	3-4

Stage	Opponents	Home	Away	Agg
	1983-84			
Round 1	Odense BK	5-0	1-0	6-0
Round 2	Atletico Bilbao	0-0	1-0	1-0
Quarter-Final	Benfica	1-0	4-1	5-1
Semi-Final	Dinamo Bucharest	1-0	2-1	3-1
Final	AS Roma	—	—	1-1

Liverpool won 4-2 on penalties

Stage	Opponents	Home	Away	Agg
	1984-85			
Round 1	Lech Poznan	4-0	1-0	5-0
Round 2	Benfica	3-1	0-1	3-2
Quarter-Final	FK Austria	4-1	1-1	5-2
Semi-Final	Panathinaikos	4-0	1-0	5-0
Final	Juventus	—	—	0-1

EUROPEAN CUP WINNERS' CUP

Even though they reached the Final first time out, the Cup Winners' Cup is the least successful European competition in Liverpool's history.

Stage	Opponents	Home	Away	Agg
1965-66				
Round 1	Juventus	2-0	0-1	2-1
Round 2	Standard Liege	3-1	2-1	5-2
Quarter-Final	Honved	2-0	0-0	2-0
Semi-Final	Celtic	2-0	0-1	2-1
Final	Borussia Dortmund	—	—	1-2
1971-72				
Round 1	Servette Geneva	2-0	1-2	3-2
Round 2	Bayern Munich	0-0	1-3	1-3
1974-75				
Round 1	Stromsgodset	11-0	1-0	12-0
Round 2	Ferencvaros	1-1	0-0	1-1

Liverpool lost on away goals

Stage	Opponents	Home	Away	Agg
1992-93				
Round 1	Apollon Limassol	6-1	2-1	8-2
Round 2	Spartak Moscow	0-2	2-4	2-6

Stage	Opponents	Home	Away	Agg
1996-97				
Round 1	MyPa	3-1	1-0	4-1
Round 2	Sion	6-3	2-1	8-4
Quarter-Final	Brann	3-0	1-1	4-1
Semi-Final	Paris St Germain	2-0	0-3	2-3

INTER-CITIES FAIRS/UEFA CUP

The Anfield boardroom has twice been the home for this trophy, competed for by high-ranking teams Europe-wide.

Stage	Opponents	Home	Away	Agg
1967-68				
Round 1	Malmo FF	2-1	2-0	4-1
Round 2	Munich 1860	8-0	1-2	9-2
Round 3	Ferencvaros	0-1	0-1	0-2
1968-69				
Round 1	Atletico Bilbao	2-1	1-2	3-3
Bilbao won on the toss of a coin				
1969-70				
Round 1	Dundalk	10-0	4-0	14-0
Round 2	Vitória Setúbal	3-2	0-1	3-3
Liverpool lost on away goals				
1970-71				
Round 1	Ferencvaros	1-0	1-1	2-1
Round 2	Dinamo Bucharest	3-0	1-1	4-1
Round 3	Hibernian	2-0	1-0	3-0
Quarter-Final	Bayern Munich	3-0	1-1	4-1
Semi-Final	Leeds Utd	0-1	0-0	0-1

Stage	Opponents	Home	Away	Agg
	1972-73			
Round 1	Eintracht Frankfurt	2-0	0-0	2-0
Round 2	AEK Athens	3-0	3-1	6-1
Round 3	Dynamo Berlin	3-1	0-0	3-1
Quarter-Final	Dynamo Dresden	2-0	1-0	3-0
Semi-Final	Tottenham H	1-0	1-2	2-2
	Liverpool won on away goals			
Final	B Moenchengladbach	3-0	0-2	3-2
	1975-76			
Round 1	Hibernian	3-1	0-1	3-2
Round 2	Real Sociedad	6-0	3-1	9-1
Round 3	Slask Wroclaw	3-0	2-1	5-1
Quarter-Final	Dynamo Dresden	2-1	0-0	2-1
Semi-Final	Barcelona	1-1	1-0	2-1
Final	FC Bruges	3-2	1-1	4-3
	1991-92			
Round 1	Kuusysi	6-1	0-1	6-2
Round 2	Auxerre	3-0	0-2	3-2
Round 3	Tirol	4-0	2-0	6-0
Quarter-Final	Genoa	1-2	0-2	1-4
	1995-96			
Round 1	Spartak Vladikavkaz	0-0	2-1	2-1
Round 2	Brondby	0-1	0-0	0-1
	1997-98			
Round 1	Celtic	0-0	2-2	2-2
	Liverpool won on away goals			
Round 2	Strasbourg	2-0	0-3	2-3

Liverpool's record against European opposition				
Country	**P**	**W**	**D**	**L**	**F-A**
---	---	---	---	---	---
Austria	4	3	1	—	11-2
Belgium	7	6	1	—	14-5
Bulgaria	4	3	—	1	7-3
Cyprus	2	2	—	—	8-2
Denmark	4	2	1	1	6-1
Eire	4	4	—	—	19-1
England	6	1	2	3	2-5
Finland	10	7	1	2	34-6
France	8	4	—	4	10-10
Germany (East)	8	5	2	1	14-5
Gemany (West)	19	6	8	5	30-16
Greece	4	4	—	—	11-1
Holland	4	1	2	1	8-11
Hungary	8	2	4	2	5-4
Iceland	2	2	—	—	11-1
Italy	8	2	1	5	7-11
Luxemburg	2	1	1	—	3-1
Northern Ireland	2	2	—	—	7-0
Norway	4	3	1	—	16-1
Poland	6	5	—	1	13-5
Portugal	8	6	—	2	17-8
Romania	7	5	1	1	12-5
Russia	6	2	1	3	6-11
Scotland	10	6	2	2	15-5
Spain	9	6	2	1	16-5
Sweden	2	2	—	—	4-1
Switzerland	6	5	—	1	17-7
Turkey	2	1	—	1	3-1
Yugoslavia	2	—	—	2	2-4

SUBSTITUTES

Substitutes were first allowed in the mid 1960s, initially for injury only. The current game, with three subs for Premiership games and more for European ties, allows a flexibility Roy Evans is only too happy to use.

Think of famous Liverpool substitutes and only one name springs to mind – David Fairclough. The original 'super-sub', Fairclough leapt off the bench to rescue Liverpool so many times in the 1970s you lost count. He was a secret weapon, held back in case things were going wrong. The opposition knew what he was capable of but were powerless to stop him turning games Liverpool's way as he employed his fresh legs against fast-tiring defenders.

It all began in 1975-76 when Fairclough had just broken into the squad and he scored both goals in a 2-0 defeat of Burnley after coming on as a substitute. He repeated the trick in the next game with the winner in a 1-0 Merseyside derby win over Everton, and again came off the bench to score the fifth as Stoke were beaten 5-3 a fortnight later. A legend was born. He would have been a first-team regular at any other club, especially after he clinched victory against St Etienne in the following season's European Cup Quarter-Final after replacing John Toshack.

Fairclough has not been Liverpool's only match-winning substitute, however, as one of the club's most famous goalscorers of all time, Ian Rush, repeated the feat in the 1989 FA Cup Final against Everton. Rush replaced John Aldridge and scored twice in extra-time to give the Reds the trophy 3-2.

Liverpool's first-ever substitute was utility man Geoff Strong, who came on for Chris Lawler in the League game against West Ham in September 1965 – and scored the equaliser in a 1-1 draw! It wasn't so much an inspired Shankly substitution as necessitated by injury, but since the Hammers had been humbled 5-1 earlier that month (due to a freak in the fixtures computer they played both games within 9 days) it certainly helped prevent the Londoners getting their revenge.

DREAM TEAM 3

**Liverpool's most recent trophy was the 1995
Coca-Cola Cup, won with a 2-1 victory
over Bolton Wanderers.**

JAMES
1

BABB
5

RUDDOCK
6

SCALES
4

JONES
2

BARNES
10

BJORNEBYE
3

REDKNAPP
8

McMANAMAN
7

FOWLER
11

RUSH
9

LIVERPOOL

Goalkeeper **David James**

James arrived from Watford for £1.2 million in 1992. He struggled at first to displace Bruce Grobbelaar, but has since established himself as one of the most reliable keepers in the top flight and has earned England recognition despite some worrying lapses of concentration.

Right-back **Rob Jones**

Jones is generally regarded as Graeme Souness's best purchase. Bought from Crewe Alexandra for £300,000 in September 1991, Jones made an impressive debut against Manchester United and picked up a Cup winner's medal at the end of the season. Has played for England but injuries have hampered his progress.

Left-back **Stig-Inge Bjornebye**

Norwegian defender Bjornebye took time to settle at Anfield, but his defensive qualities allied to his attacking instincts and excellent dead-ball skills have made him a vital part of the Liverpool team.

Central defender **John Scales**

Scales arrived at Anfield in 1994 and looked every inch a Liverpool player, but with competition fierce only stayed at the club a couple of years before being transferred to Tottenham.

Central defender   Phil Babb

Babb arrived at the same time as Scales, and took time to become a fixture in the Liverpool line-up. The classy defender plays international football for the Republic of Ireland.

Central defender   Neil Ruddock

Ruddock was criticised for being overweight during his early career at Anfield, but he worked hard at the problem with a club dietician and became a firm favourite of the Liverpool crowd.

Midfielder   Steve McManaman

McManaman won an FA Cup winner's medal in 1992, producing a memorable performance against Sunderland. He was again the star at Wembley, scoring both the goals that beat Bolton. He is a player of immense talent and is important to both Liverpool and England.

Midfielder   Jamie Redknapp

Redknapp is a stylish midfielder who has also played for England. A fine passer of the ball with a powerful shot, he has struggled with injuries recently.

Striker   Ian Rush

Rush's last medal of a glittering Liverpool career was this League Cup success. He is a player whose goalscoring feats have set the standard for the latest crop of strikers to try and emulate.

Midfielder   John Barnes

Barnes burst on to Anfield with a series of glittering displays that inspired Liverpool to the Championship. He suffered from injuries towards the end of his Liverpool days, but still made a vital contribution in a more withdrawn role.

Striker   Robbie Fowler

Fowler may be the man to break all of Ian Rush's goalscoring records if he continues at his current rate. He reached the 100-goal milestone quicker than his mentor and his ability in front of goal is unquestioned.

WORST SEASON 3

Liverpool's worst season of recent times was the 1993-94 campaign. This was for more than just statistical reasons, even though they finished eighth, their lowest position since they returned to the top flight in 1962-63. Other reasons included poor performances and the position of manager Graeme Souness, which finally became untenable in the January.

Despite winning their first three matches, Liverpool lost three of the next four, including home defeats by Tottenham and Blackburn. Discipline was also disappearing, with Rob Jones sent off at Coventry and Bruce Grobbelaar and Steve McManaman lucky not to receive a similar fate in the Merseyside derby after fighting with each other. Neil Ruddock and Julian Dicks were added to the defence and Nigel Clough's early form petered out.

Liverpool picked up no points in September and had already used 20 players. They went five games without scoring and there were problems with injuries, something which had not plagued the Liverpool teams of the previous 20 years. Souness had changed the club's training methods to those he had learned in Italy. There was also a huge turnover of players, and some of those Souness had discarded came back to haunt him – particularly Barry Venison, Peter Beardsley and Mike Hooper in a 3-0 defeat at Newcastle.

As Liverpool produced some tepid displays at home, alleviated only briefly by a memorable 3-3 draw at home to

Manchester United, Souness's time was running out. The final straw was an FA Cup Third Round replay at home to First Division Bristol City, where Liverpool almost surrendered to lose 1-0 and crash out of the competition.

With the Kop turning on their manager, an unusual situation in the extreme, Souness was sacked – the first to be dismissed in over 30 years. Assistant Roy Evans took over in a return to the old Liverpool method of doing things, but he could do little to improve the season, presiding over nine defeats in his 16 matches to the end of the campaign including a 1-0 defeat at home to Norwich in what was the last match played before the Kop was knocked down to be replaced with a new stand. Evans however changed the squad and gradually created a team capable of challenging for honours once again.

1993-94 LEAGUE RECORD

Opponents	Home	Away
Arsenal	0-0	0-1
Aston Villa	2-1	1-2
Blackburn Rovers	0-1	0-2
Chelsea	2-1	0-1
Coventry City	1-0	0-1
Everton	2-1	0-2
Ipswich Town	1-0	2-1
Leeds United	2-0	0-2
Manchester City	2-1	0-0
Manchester United	3-3	0-1
Newcastle United	0-2	0-3
Norwich City	0-1	2-2
Oldham Athletic	2-1	3-0
Queens Park Rangers	3-2	3-1
Sheffield United	1-2	0-0
Sheffield Wednesday	2-0	1-3
Southampton	4-2	2-4
Swindon Town	2-2	5-0
Tottenham Hotspur	1-2	3-3
West Ham United	2-0	2-1
Wimbledon	1-1	1-1

ANFIELD'S ALL-TIME ROLL OF HONOUR

1893-94	Division Two Champions
1895-96	Division Two Champions
1898-99	Division One Runners-up
1900-01	Division One Champions
1904-05	Division Two Champions
1905-06	Division One Champions
1909-10	Division One Runners-up
1913-14	FA Cup Runners-up
1921-22	Division One Champions
1922-23	Division One Champions
1946-47	Division One Champions
1949-50	FA Cup Runners-up
1961-62	Division Two Champions
1963-64	Division One Champions
1964-65	FA Cup Winners
1965-66	Division One Champions and European Cup Winners' Cup Runners-up
1968-69	Division One Runners-up
1970-71	FA Cup Runners-up
1972-73	Division One Champions and UEFA Cup Winners
1973-74	Division One Runners-up and FA Cup Winners
1974-75	Division One Runners-up
1975-76	Division One Champions and UEFA Cup Winners

1976-77	Division One Champions, FA Cup Runners-up, European Cup Winners and European Super Cup Winners
1977-78	Division One Runners-up, League Cup Runners-up and European Cup Winners
1978-79	Division One Champions
1979-80	Division One Champions
1980-81	League Cup Winners, European Cup Winners and World Club Championship Runners-up
1981-82	Division One Champions and League Cup Winners
1982-83	Division One Champions and League Cup Winners
1983-84	Division One Champions, League Cup Winners and European Cup Winners
1984-85	Division One Runners-up and European Cup Runners-up
1985-86	Division One Champions, FA Cup Winners and League Super Cup Winners
1986-87	Division One Runners-up and League Cup Runners-up
1987-88	Division One Champions and FA Cup Runners-up
1988-89	Division One Runners-up and FA Cup Winners
1989-90	Division One Champions
1990-91	Division One Runners-up
1991-92	FA Cup Winners
1994-95	League Cup Winners
1995-96	FA Cup Runners-up

QUIZ ANSWERS

See page 122-125 for questions.

1   Steve Ogrizovic.

2   Dean Saunders. His father Roy played for the club
     in the 1950s.

3   David Speedie.

4   Sheffield Wednesday.

5   Crewe Alexandra.

6   Nottingham Forest.

7   He was in prison for a driving offence.

8   Thirteen.

9   Jack Balmer in 1946.

10   Jamie Redknapp.

11   Manchester City, 6-0 in the League and 4-0 in
     the League Cup.

12   Ferencvaros in the Fairs Cup, 1967-68.

13   John Wark.

14   Mike Marsh and David Burrows.

15   Phil Thompson.

16   Portsmouth.

17   Gary Gillespie.

18   Graeme Souness and Terry McDermott.

19   John Scales and Phil Babb.

20   Peter Beardsley.

21   Smith scored with a header from an indirect free-kick, but the Liverpool defence didn't think Smith had touched the ball.

22   Celtic.

23   Jimmy Melia.

24   Everton twice, Nottingham Forest and Wimbledon.

25   Five.

26   3-0 to Liverpool.

27   Gordon Hodgson.

28   Mark Walters.

29   Nigeria.

30   Southampton.

31   Five.

32   Melwood.

33   Coventry City.

34   SV Hamburg.

35   Five.

36   Gerry and the Pacemakers.

37   John Aldridge and Ray Houghton.

38   5,000.

39   Steve Heighway.

40   Jan Molby and John Toshack.

THE LAST WORD

'Some people believe football is a matter of life and death. I am very disappointed with that attitude. I can assure you it is much, much more important than that.'

Bill Shankly